Fairy Tale Knits

32 Projects to Knit Happily Ever After

Fairy Tale Knits

32 Projects to Knit Happily Ever After

~ by ~

Alison Stewart-Guinee

WILEY

Wiley Publishing, Inc.

Fairy Tale Knits: 32 Projects to Knit Happily Ever After

Copyright © 2009 by Wiley Publishing, Inc., Hoboken, New Jersey. All rights reserved.

Published by Wiley Publishing, Inc., Hoboken, New Jersey

For general information on our other products and services or to obtain technical support please contact our Customer Care Department within the U.S. at (877) 762-2974, outside the U.S. at (317) 572-3993 or fax (317) 572-4002.

Wiley also publishes its books in a variety of electronic formats. Some content that appears in print may not be available in electronic books. For more information about Wiley products, please visit our web site at www.wiley.com.

Library of Congress Cataloging-in-Publication Data

Stewart-Guinee, Alison, 1964–
  Fairy tale knits : 32 projects to knit happily ever after / by Alison Stewart-Guinee.
       p. cm.
  ISBN-13: 978-0-470-26268-9
  ISBN-10: 0-470-26268-0
  1. Knitting--Patterns. 2. Fairy tales in art. I. Title.
  TT825.S738 2009
  746.43'2041—dc22

Printed in the United States of America

10   9   8   7   6   5   4   3   2   1

Book production by Wiley Publishing, Inc., Composition Services

Credits

Acquisitions Editor
Roxane Cerda

Project Editor
Donna Wright

Copy Editor
Carol Pogoni

Technical Editor
Sharon Turner

Editorial Manager
Christina Stambaugh

Publisher
Cindy Kitchel

**Vice President and
Executive Publisher**
Kathy Nebenhaus

Interior Design
Elizabeth Brooks

Photography
Matt Bowen

Acknowledgments

There are so many people who helped make this book a reality. Writing it has been a dream come true and it wouldn't have been possible without all of you.

To the good folks at Wiley, thank you for taking a chance on this first-time author and for all the behind the scenes time spent on this book. Thanks especially to senior editor Roxane Cerda, for believing in this project from the beginning and for holding my hand through the entire process. It has been a wonderful journey. Many thanks go to the talented Sharon Turner for her excellent technical editing skills and generous spirit. Your insight and words of encouragement have been invaluable. Thanks as well to project editor Donna Wright for pulling it all together and seeing this book through to the end. Grateful acknowledgement goes to photographer Matt Bowen for his wonderful photos and for making the photo shoots fun. Thanks also to Jodi Bratch for photo styling and assistance. To all of the beautiful models whose faces grace these pages, and to their families for jumping in with such enthusiasm, thank you. You made the designs and the fairy tale come to life.

There aren't words enough to express my gratitude to my family. You have graciously put up with boxes of yarn, my prattling on about knitting and my eventual disappearance to finish this book. Thank you for being my loudest cheerleaders, for your support, love, and laughter. To my husband, Dave Guinee, thank you for providing a wealth of encouragement, precious time, and, not the least, for always being there. I couldn't do it without you. To my children, Mallory, Brockman, and Liam, thank you for your patience and enthusiasm for this project, for keeping me smiling and for being the generous, loving souls that you are.

To my mother, Polly Stewart, thank you for introducing me to the joys of crafting, for always believing in me, and for lovely moments of creating together. To Susan Hahn, thank you for walks, talks, and true friendship. Many thanks go to Suzanne Halvorson, a wonderful mentor and friend. To knitting friends far and near, I thank you for sharing your beautiful work, invigorating conversation, and your love of this craft. You inspire me.

*This book is lovingly dedicated to my husband Dave
and to my muses, Mallory, Brockman, and Liam*

Table of Contents

Introduction

nitting for children is a singular pleasure. It is an invitation to infuse your work with a sense of play, an opportunity to create a gift of love that is both functional and fanciful. Because designs for little ones are small and relatively quick to knit, they are ideal projects for knitterly experimentation and exploration. Interesting design details—trims and edgings, which might overwhelm other projects—are just right for creating appealing children's designs. These little details are fun to knit, and they add an element of whimsy to the finished piece. It is this aspect of play that makes knitting for kids so enjoyable.

This collection includes clothing, accessories, and decorative items created to fit into the daily life of a child. Light-hearted and practical, these designs are intended to delight the imagination and inspire creative play in the children who wear them. There can be no greater reward for your knitting endeavors than that.

When my children were little, I made princess dresses, capes, wizard robes, armor, and more. The requests usually came in something like this, "Mom, could you make me a … but I want it to look like this … and can it have a … ?" I made countless outfits to their exacting standards and loved every minute of it. I thought of these outfits as costumes, but soon realized that my children saw them as clothes. These were the things that they wanted to wear.

As adults we look for clothes that fit our lifestyle, suit our profession, are comfortable, and reflect our sense of style. The pieces in this collection are designed for the work of children—imagination and creative play. They are not costumes, but rather outfits to wear on a regular basis.

Mirror, Mirror on the Wall

Fairy tales are the perfect source of inspiration for children's designs. The characters in these classic stories are larger than life, and their adventures are an ideal place for children to explore their hopes and dreams. The fairy tale world is a place where a child can be a princess one moment and a pirate the next. In designing for children, I strive to create comfortable clothes and useful accessories that fit into that world of imagination. I like to incorporate details that invoke storybook characters but try to avoid heavy-handed and contrived designs. It is my aim to create patterns that transition easily between the fantasy world of a child and "real life."

Fairy Tale Knitting

The projects in this book are for knitters of all abilities, from beginner to advanced. The garments are offered in a range of sizes for infants to 8 year olds and are made in a variety of yarn weights and textures. The suggested yarns are soft, durable, and easy to maintain. The designs are made with simple shaping and seamless-construction techniques. This is a straightforward, commonsense approach to knitting that works especially well for children's garments. It has its roots in traditional folk knitting; like the folk tales reflected in these designs, it has stood the test of time. It is a method that maximizes the knitting and minimizes the finishing. Most knitters love this method of knitting. For those who prefer to make these patterns as pieced projects, I have included simple instructions for converting the designs.

Each pattern begins with an overview outlining the techniques used and the basic construction of the project. Special stitch patterns and charts are included within each pattern. At the back of the book, you will find three appendices that cover the abbreviations, basic knitting skills, and the colorwork, felting, embellishing, and finishing techniques used in this book.

Seamless Construction

Many of the projects in this book rely on seamless-construction techniques. In seamless designs, knitting and construction are intertwined. Projects are created sculpturally, as whole cloth. Instead of making separate pieces of fabric for the individual components of a garment and then sewing the pieces together, seamless designs are worked in as few pieces as possible. For example, the body of a sweater is worked as one single piece, in the round, in rows or in a combination of both. After the body is complete, stitches are picked up along the edges of the piece for the sleeves and collar. The sleeves and collar are completed seamlessly from these edges. Once the knitting is complete, all that remains is weaving in the ends, blocking, and embellishment.

As a designer of children's wear, I find this method particularly appealing. Children have specific requirements when it comes to clothes. Their clothes must weather days of play and endure yanking, pulling, and stretching. Outfits need to be comfortable, sturdy, and off the needles before the next growth spurt.

One of the really wonderful qualities of a knitted garment is that it can bend and stretch with the body, perfect for active, growing children. In a seamlessly knit sweater, there are no seams to rip when the sweater is pulled too vigorously, there are no bulky edges inside, and there is very little finishing after the garment is off the needles.

Converting Seamless Designs

If seamless knitting isn't for you, that's okay, too. I really believe that there is no one right way to knit, and you should feel free to knit these projects in the way that works best for you.

Most of the patterns in this book can easily be converted. Simply go through the pattern and work each sweater section (back, front, and sleeves) separately, adding an extra stitch to each side of the piece for the seam. Work the seam stitches in stockinette stitch. Keep in mind the stitch orientation when converting stitch patterns. For example, to convert stockinette stitch from knitting in the round to flat knitting you will need to purl every other row instead of knitting all rounds. After the knitting is complete, block the pieces. Seam pieces together as you would normally, shoulders together first, then sleeves to body, and finally underarm and side seams. Sweater bands and collars should be worked according to the pattern instructions, by picking up stitches and knitting them directly onto the piece after the shoulder seams have been worked.

Knit these patterns however you want. What's most important is that you knit in the way that makes sense to you and feels right. Either way, seamed or not, these patterns are fun to knit and will be an adorable addition to your child's wardrobe.

Gauge—Do I Really Have to Make a Swatch?

When I first started knitting, I hated making gauge swatches. It felt like something I was supposed to do, like having to eat your vegetables or doing homework. I saw it as this big thing standing between me and knitting bliss.

In those early years, I threw caution to the wind and started many projects with only a rough idea what my gauge was. I knew I was a loose knitter so I would move a size down from the suggested needle size and start on my merry way. For some projects this was okay, scarves and blankets were fine—for the most part— but many of my hand-knits were wildly off and ended up abandoned at the back of a closet. The upside of all those ill-fitting knits was that I started designing my own sweaters, and designing got me swatching. Instead of being something I had to do before I could begin knitting, it became part of the knitting process. Now, I think of it as the first step to discovering what the yarn and I can do together.

When you sit down to knit your swatch, just remember that no stitch is ever wasted. These little bits of knitting provide invaluable information and have many other uses as well. I was thrilled the first time one of my children asked if he could keep the gauge swatch for the sweater I was knitting. In the years since, our family has found that swatches can be repurposed for all sorts of things. In addition to being a promise of the cozy knit to come, these little squares make great doll blankets, bags for little treasures, dollhouse furnishings, pockets, decorative patches, coasters, wrist warmers, hats, and more. Always loath to lose time or yarn, I often find it helpful to plan my swatch around a specific little project. Usually, my kids have great ideas for these squares of knitting.

How to Make a Gauge Swatch

Look to your pattern to determine the stitch, yarn, and needle size for the project. The gauge section of the patterns in this book will advise you of the specific number of stitches to make a 4" (10cm) square of knitting. Divide the number by 4 to get the number of stitches in 1" (3cm). Cast on enough stitches to make a 5" (13cm) square of knitting. This will allow you to measure your gauge without having to measure the swatch edges, thereby providing a more accurate result. After you have *swatched* in the stitch pattern specified in your pattern for about 5" (13cm), bind off. Block the swatch (see page 159). This will give you a good idea of how the fabric will behave after washing and finishing.

Once the swatch is dry, lay it on a table and use a ruler to measure how many stitches and rows are in 4" (10cm). Refer to the pattern to see if you are getting the required gauge.

Getting Gauge

If you have more stitches per 4" (10cm) than the pattern recommends, then your gauge is tighter than the required gauge and you should switch to a larger size needle and try again.

If you have fewer stitches per 4" (10cm) than the pattern recommends, then your gauge is looser than the required gauge and you should try again with a smaller size needle.

Occasionally, you may find that your stitch gauge is correct but your row gauge is off. It is generally more important that your stitch gauge is correct. For most of the projects in this book, the length of a piece is determined by measurements in inches not by number of rows.

Swatching in the Round

For projects that are worked in the round, it is important that the gauge swatch is also worked in the round. To do this, find the recommended gauge in the pattern. This will give you the number of stitches per 4" (10cm) of knitting. Multiply that number by two to get the number of stitches for your gauge swatch. Using a double-pointed needle (the size noted in the gauge section of the pattern), cast on stitches for your gauge swatch, place a marker, join in the round, and work in pattern for 5" (13cm). Bind off and block the gauge swatch. Measure the swatch as above to determine your gauge.

Swatching for Projects with Circular and Flat Knitting

Some of the patterns in this book use both flat and circular knitting techniques in the body of the piece. Pullover sweaters and dresses fall in this category. In these patterns, the knitting begins in the round and is divided for front and back at the armholes. It is important that you achieve the required gauge when working both sections. To swatch for these projects, you can either make two separate swatches (one in the round and one flat) or make one swatch that has a section worked flat and a section worked in the round. To make a single swatch for both circular and flat knitting, cast on stitches as you would to make a swatch in the round. Work for 5" (13cm), bind-off half of the swatch stitches and work the remainder of the swatch (another 5" [13cm]) back and forth in rows. If you find that your stitch count is not the same in both sections, move your needle size up or down to achieve the recommended gauge and uniform knitting. Most of the time this isn't an issue, but occasionally a knitter will have to change the needle size used in one section or the other to maintain the same gauge.

Knitting Happily Ever After ...

It is my hope that you will find within these pages designs that please the little ones in your life and inspire your own creativity. They are a starting point, and I encourage you to make them your own. Small and quick, kid knits are the perfect palette for creative exploration. Ask your kids for their input (or if they are like mine they've probably already piped up) and let them get involved. You'll find that they take pride in the little details that they help design. Add a bobble here, embroider a bit there and soon your child's closet will be filled with one-of-a-kind treasures.

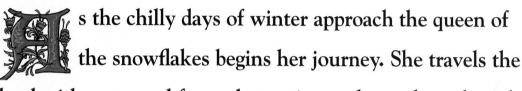

Snow Queen

As the chilly days of winter approach the queen of the snowflakes begins her journey. She travels the land with snow and frost, decorating each tree branch with glittering ice crystals and covering the earth in a blanket of white. When winter brings her to your door, your little one will stay cozy and warm in this elegant ensemble.

Coat

Knit in luscious alpaca, this lovely sweater coat is soft as a cloud and warm enough to keep out the coldest chill. Vintage styling and delicate lacey details give this coat the look of a treasured family heirloom. Put it together with the fluffy fur capelet and reversible muff to create an outfit that's truly fit for a queen.

Capelet

This fluffy confection is the perfect winter wrap, dressy enough for holiday celebrations and comfy enough for school and play. It looks darling on little ones from 18 months to 8 years old. Made in soft faux fur, this capelet will keep your child snug for years to come.

Muff

Your little girl will feel like a princess with her hands tucked inside this toasty hand warmer. It is completely reversible, soft fur on one side and wooly alpaca felt with fur trim on the other. With two layers of warmth built in, this muff is a cozy alternative to traditional mittens and gloves and is perfect for protecting little mitts from winter's icy chill.

Coat

Although this pattern may look complicated, it's actually quite easy. The simple pattern repeat of the skirt and minimal shaping of this design make for uncomplicated and enjoyable knitting. The skirt is worked in German Herringbone stitch, an easily memorized six-row pattern repeat, and is shaped with a row of decreases at the bodice edge. The stockinette stitch bodice is worked to the underarms, where the piece is divided for the left front, the back, and the right front. Each section is then worked separately to the shoulders. Once the shoulder seams are complete, the sleeves are worked in the round from armhole to cuff. A simple eyelet ruffle trims the sleeves and the coat collar.

SIZES
1–2 years (2–4 years, 4–6 years)

FINISHED MEASUREMENTS
Chest: 24 (26, 28)" [61 (66, 71)cm]
Length from hem to shoulder: 22$\frac{1}{2}$ (25$\frac{1}{2}$, 28$\frac{1}{2}$)" [57 (65, 72)cm]

Sample size 4–6 years

MATERIALS
Plymouth *Baby Alpaca Worsted* (100% baby alpaca; 102 yd. [93m] per 50g skein): #6074 Robin's Egg Blue, 7 (9, 11) skeins
US 7 (4.5mm) 16" circular needle
US 7 (4.5mm) 24" circular needle

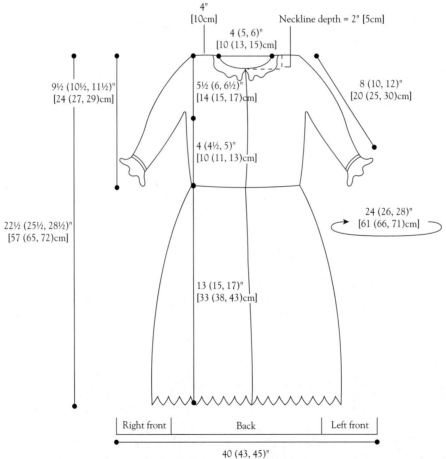

4"
[10cm]

Neckline depth = 2" [5cm]

4 (5, 6)"
[10 (13, 15)cm]

9$\frac{1}{2}$ (10$\frac{1}{2}$, 11$\frac{1}{2}$)"
[24 (27, 29)cm]

5$\frac{1}{2}$ (6, 6$\frac{1}{2}$)"
[14 (15, 17)cm]

8 (10, 12)"
[20 (25, 30)cm]

4 (4$\frac{1}{2}$, 5)"
[10 (11, 13)cm]

24 (26, 28)"
[61 (66, 71)cm]

22$\frac{1}{2}$ (25$\frac{1}{2}$, 28$\frac{1}{2}$)"
[57 (65, 72)cm]

13 (15, 17)"
[33 (38, 43)cm]

| Right front | Back | Left front |

40 (43, 45)"
[102 (109, 114)cm]

US 7 (4.5mm) double-pointed needles
US 5 (3.75mm) 16" circular needle
US 5 (3.75mm) double-pointed needles
Stitch markers
Row counter
2 stitch holders
Tapestry needle
1/2" (1cm) buttons—4
1 yd. (1m) of 1/2" (1cm) ribbon (optional)

GAUGE

20 sts and 26 rows = 4" (10cm) in St st using US 7 (4.5mm) needles, or size needed to obtain gauge
24 sts and 26 rows = 4" (10cm) in German Herringbone stitch using US 7 (4.5mm) needles, or size needed to obtain gauge.

STITCH PATTERNS

German Herringbone stitch worked flat—(multiple of 15 sts plus 2; 6-row rep)
Row 1 (RS): P2, *M1, k3, p2, p3tog, p2, k3, M1, p2; rep from * across.
Row 2: *K2, p4, k5, p4; rep from * across, end k2.
Row 3: P2, *M1, k4, p1, p3tog, p1, k4, M1, p2; rep from * across.
Row 4: *K2, p5, k3, p5; rep from * across, end k2.
Row 5: P2, *M1, k5, p3tog, k5, M1, p2; rep from * across.
Row 6: *K2, p6, k1, p6; rep from * across, end k2.
Stockinette stitch worked flat—Knit on RS rows; purl on WS rows.
Stockinette stitch worked in the round—Knit all stitches every round.
Cable cast on (page 146)
K2tog (page 149)
P2tog tbl (page 150)
P3tog (page 150)
Ssk (page 150)
M1 (page 149)
Yo (page 148)

SPECIAL TECHNIQUES

Three-needle bind-off (page 151)
Picot bind-off (see instructions in this pattern)

Instructions

Coat Skirt

NOTE: Cast on the number of stitches below as follows: CO 2, pm, *CO 15, pm; rep from * while casting on the number of stitches below. Placing markers after every fifteenth stitch will help keep the patt straight and make correcting mistakes easier.

With US 7 24" circular needle, CO 242 (257, 272) sts.

Beg with Row 1, work German Herringbone stitch for a total of 72 (84, 96) rows—12 (14, 16) six-row repeats. You may want to use a row counter to keep track of the patt.

Next row (RS): P2, *k6, p1, k6, p2; rep from * across.
Gather skirt (WS): *P2tog; rep from * across row to end for sizes 1–2 and 4–6, for size 2–4 only end p1—121 (129, 136) sts. Do not cut yarn.

Bodice

Work bodice in St st for 4 (4½, 5)" [10 (11, 13)cm] from the upper edge of the skirt, ending with a WS row.

Divide for Armholes

Right Front

With RS facing, knit across the first 29 (31, 33) sts of the row. These stitches form the right front. Do not cut yarn.

Put rem stitches, for the sweater back and left front, on a spare needle or holder to be worked later.

Next row (WS): P29 (31, 33) sts from right armhole edge to right front opening. Continue working in St st on the right front stitches only for 3½ (4, 4½)" [9 (10, 11)cm], ending with a WS row. You will be working from the center front opening to the armhole edge on RS rows and from the armhole to the center opening on WS rows.

Right Neckline Shaping

Row 1 (RS): BO 3 (4, 5) sts at neck edge, k to armhole—26 (27, 28) sts.

Row 2: Purl to last 3 sts, p2tog tbl, p1—25 (26, 27) sts.

Row 3: K1, ssk, k to end of row—24 (25, 26) sts.

Rows 4 and 5: Rep Rows 2 and 3—22 (23, 24) sts.

Row 6: Purl.

Row 7: K1, ssk, k to end of row—21 (22, 23) sts.

Rows 8 and 9: Rep Rows 6 and 7—20 (21, 22) sts.

Work without further shaping in St st until armhole opening measures 5½ (6, 6½)" [14 (15, 17)cm], ending with a WS row. Cut yarn and put rem shoulder stitches on a holder.

Back

With RS facing, slip the 63 (67, 70) sts for the sweater back off of the holder and onto the 24" US 7 circular needle, leaving the rem 29 (31, 33) sts for the left front on the holder for later. Join yarn and beg with a RS row, work sweater back in St st until the armhole opening measures 5½ (6, 6½)" [14 (15, 17)cm], ending with a WS row. Cut yarn, leaving stitches on 24" needle.

Left Front

Slip rem 29 (31, 33) sts from the holder onto the 16" US 7 needle. Beg with RS facing, join yarn at left armhole edge and knit to center front opening.

You will be working from the armhole edge to the center front opening on all RS rows and from the center front opening to the armhole on all WS rows.

Continue to work on left front in St st for 3½ (4, 4½)" [9 (10, 11)cm], ending with a RS row.

Left Neckline Shaping

Row 1 (WS): BO 3 (4, 5) sts at left neckline edge, p to armhole—26 (27, 28) sts.

Row 2: K to last 3 sts, k2tog, k1—25 (26, 27) sts.

Row 3: P1, p2tog, p to end—24 (25, 26) sts.

Rows 4 and 5: Rep Rows 2 and 3—22 (23, 24) sts.

Row 6: Knit.

Row 7: P1, p2tog, p to end—21 (22, 23) sts.

Rows 8 and 9: Rep Rows 6 and 7—20 (21, 22) sts.

Work without further shaping in St st until armhole opening measures 5½ (6, 6½)" [14 (15, 17)cm], ending with a WS row. Cut yarn and put rem shoulder stitches on a holder.

Shoulder Seams

With the 63 (67, 70) sts for the sweater back on the 24" US 7 needle, place the 20 (21, 22) sts for the right and left fronts on two separate US 7 dpns. Turn the coat inside out so that the RS of the work are together. Beg at the left armhole, with the back of the sweater facing you. Holding the dpn and circular needle parallel to one another, join yarn and use the 16" US 7 needle to work a three-needle bind-off across the stitches of the left shoulder, joining the stitches for the left front and the back together. Do not cut yarn. After working across the 20 (21, 22) sts for the left shoulder, continue to work across the rem stitches for the sweater back as follows. Knit (do not BO) the next 22 (24, 25) sts for the back of the neck. After knitting the stitches for the back of the neck, work a three-needle bind-off across the rem 20 (21, 22) sts for the right shoulder. Cut yarn and fasten off. Leave the 23 (25, 26) live sts rem for back of the neck on the circular needle.

Sleeves

The sleeves are worked in St st in the round from the armhole edge. To begin you will pick up stitches along the armhole edge with RS of work facing and beg at the center underarm. Both sleeves are worked the same way, so you can work them in the order you choose.

With US 5 dpns, RS facing, and beg at the underarm, pick up 54 (58, 62) sts evenly around the armhole edge. Pm, arrange stitches evenly on dpns, and join in the round.

Rnd 1: Knit.
Switch to US 7 dpns.
Rnds 2–4: Knit.
Rnd 5: K1, ssk, k to within 3 sts of marker, k2tog, k1—52 (56, 60) sts.

Rep last four rounds, dec 2 sts as established every fourth round 9 (10, 11) times—34 (36, 38) sts.

Work without further shaping until sleeve measures 6¼ (8¼, 10¼)" [16 (21, 26)cm] from underarm.

Cuff
Switch to US 5 dpns.
Rnd 1: Purl.
Rnd 2: Knit.
Rnds 3 and 4: Rep Rnds 1 and 2.

Ruffle Trim
Rnds 1 and 2: Knit.
Switch back to US 7 dpns.
Rnd 3: *K1, yo; rep from *, end with a yo—68 (72, 76) sts.
Rnd 4: Knit.
Rnd 5: Purl.
Rnds 6 and 7: Rep Rnds 4 and 5.

Picot Bind-Off
BO 2 sts, *sl the stitch on the RH needle back to the LH needle, CO 2 sts with a cable cast on, BO 4 sts; rep from * to end of round. Cut yarn and fasten off.

Repeat for second sleeve.

Button Band
With 16" US 5 needle, RS facing, and beg at the upper edge of the left front neck edge, pick up 35 (41, 44) sts down to the lower bodice edge (where the skirt begins).

Knit 7 rows.

BO pwise.

Buttonhole Band
With 16" US 5 needle, RS facing, and beg at bottom edge of the right front bodice, pick up 35 (41, 44) sts up to neck edge.

Knit 3 rows.

Make buttonholes (RS): *K2, k2tog, yo twice, ssk, k5 (7, 8); rep from * 3 times, end k2.
Next row: K across, knitting into the back loop of each yo from the previous row.

Knit 2 rows.

BO pwise.

Collar
With 16" US 5 circular needle, RS facing, and beg at the right front neck edge, pick up 16 (17, 18) sts to the right shoulder seam.

K across the 23 (25, 26) sts held in reserve for back of the neck and pick up 16 (17, 18) sts from the left shoulder seam down to left neck edge—55 (59, 62) sts.

Row 1 (RS of collar): Purl.
Row 2 (WS of collar): Knit.
Rows 3 and 4: Purl.
Row 5 (RS): Knit.
Switch to US 7 circular needle.
Row 6: K1, *yo, k1; rep from * to end—109 (117, 123) sts.
Rows 7–10: Knit.
Row 11: Work picot bind-off as for sleeve cuffs.

Finishing
Weave in all ends. Block piece.
If desired, sew ribbon facing onto WS of buttonhole band and button band to reinforce the center opening of the bodice (see the facing instructions on page 159). Sew buttons to button band opposite buttonholes.

Capelet

Made in soft faux fur, this capelet is worked from the neck down in garter stitch rows, with raglan shaping. After the body of the capelet is complete, stitches are picked up at the neckline, and the collar is worked in garter stitch. The closure of this capelet is formed from ribbon ties, which are sewn to the front openings of the cape and topped with decorative buttons.

SIZES
18 months–8 years

FINISHED MEASUREMENTS
Length from back of neck to hem: 13" (33cm)
Length from front collar to hem: 12" (30cm)
Width at hem: 46^1/$_2$" (118cm)

MATERIALS
Lion Brand *Tiffany* (100% nylon; 137 yd. [125m] per 50g skein): #098 Cream, 8 skeins
US 8 (5mm) 24" circular needle
Stitch markers
Row counter
Tapestry needle
Sewing needle
Sewing thread to match yarn
^{2}/$_3$ yd. (.61m) of 1" (3cm) double-sided satin ribbon
2 decorative buttons in size desired

GAUGE
16 sts and 32 rows = 4" (10cm) with double-stranded yarn in garter stitch on US 8 (5mm) needle, or size needed to obtain gauge

STITCH PATTERNS
Garter stitch worked flat—Knit all stitches every row.
Kfb (page 148)
M1 (page 149)

Instructions

Body

With two strands of yarn held together, CO 32 sts.

NOTE: The eight markers placed on Row 1 divide the fronts, the back, and the shoulder sections of the cape and mark the raglan "seam stitches." While this cape contains no actual seams, it is around these stitches that the raglan shaping occurs. There are four seam stitches, one between the right front and the right shoulder, one between the right shoulder and the back, one between the back and the left shoulder, and one between the left shoulder and the left front. An increase is worked immediately before and after each of these stitches.

Row 1: K1 (left front), pm, k1, pm, k5 (left shoulder sts), pm, k1, pm, k16 (capelet back), pm, k1, pm, k5 (right shoulder sts), pm, k1, pm, k1 (right front).

Row 2: Kfb, M1, sm, k1, sm, M1, k5, M1, sm, k1, sm, M1, k16, M1, sm, k1, sm, M1, k5, M1, sm, k1, sm, M1, kfb—42 sts.

Row 3: Knit across row, knitting into the back loop of all increases from the previous row and slipping markers as you go.

Row 4: Kfb, *k to marker, M1, sm, k1, sm, M1; rep from * 3 times, k to last st, kfb—52 sts.

Rows 5–10: Rep Rows 3 and 4—82 sts.

Row 11: Knit.

Row 12: *K to marker, M1, sm, k1, sm, M1; rep from * 3 times, k to end of row, CO 3 sts—93 sts.

Row 13: Knit across row, CO 3 sts—96 sts.

Row 14: Sl 1, *k to marker, M1, sm, k1, sm, M1; rep from * 3 times, k to end of row (8 increases)—104 sts.

Row 15: Sl 1, k across row.

Rows 16–31: Rep Rows 14 and 15—168 sts.

Row 32: Sl 1, k5, *M1, k6; rep from * to end of row—195 sts.

Row 33: Sl 1, k across row.

Row 34 and all rem rows: Rep Row 33 until front of cape measures 12" (30cm) or desired length.
BO kwise.

Collar

Beg at one of the front corners of the neck edge, pick up 52 sts along the CO edge of the cape.

Rows 1–20: Knit.
BO kwise.

Finishing

Weave in all ends.

Attach Ribbon and Buttons to Cape

Cut ribbon into two equal pieces approximately 12" (30cm) long each. Pin the ribbon to the inside edge of cape front along the neckline edge (below the collar). Position button on outside of the cape with the cape fabric sandwiched between the button and the ribbon. Sew the ribbon and the button to the cape simultaneously, going through the button, the cape, and under the backside of the ribbon. Repeat for second ribbon tie on the opposite front opening.

Muff

The construction of this muff couldn't be simpler—it is essentially a knitted tube worked in the round. The alpaca section of the muff is knitted first, in stockinette stitch. When it is complete, faux fur yarn is joined and the remainder of the muff is worked in garter stitch. A seam at the end brings the cast-on and bound-off edges together. A quick trip to the washer for felting finishes it off—plush fur on one side and dense alpaca with fur trim on the other.

FINISHED MEASUREMENTS

Before Felting
Circumference: 17" (43cm)
Width: 10$\frac{1}{2}$" (27cm)

After Felting
Circumference: 16" (41cm)
Width: 8" (20cm)

Plymouth *Baby Alpaca Worsted* (100% baby alpaca; 102 yd. [92.3m]
    per 50g skein): #6074 Robin's Egg Blue (yarn A), 2 skeins
Lion Brand Yarns *Tiffany* (100% nylon; 137 yd. [125m] per 50g ball):
    #098 Cream (yarn B), 3 skeins
US 10 (6mm) 16" circular needle
Stitch marker
Tapestry needle

GAUGE

12 sts and 18 rows = 4" (10cm) in St st with double strand of yarn A
    on US 10 (6 mm) needle, or size needed to obtain gauge
12 sts and 20 rows = 4" (10cm) in garter stitch with triple strand of
    yarn B on US 10 (6mm) needle, or size needed to obtain gauge

STITCH PATTERNS

Stockinette stitch worked in the round—Knit all stitches every
    round.
Garter stitch worked in the round—Knit a round, purl a round.

SPECIAL TECHNIQUES

Felting (page 160)

Instructions
Felted Section of Muff

With two strands of yarn A held together, CO 50 sts.
Join work in the round, taking care not to twist stitches,
and work in garter stitch for 4 rounds, ending with a purl
round.

Work in St st for 8" (20cm).
End this section of the muff by working 4 more rounds of
garter stitch, ending with a purl round. Cut yarn.

Fur Section of Muff

Beg the fur section of the muff by joining three strands of
yarn B.

Rnd 1 and all odd rnds: Knit.
Rnd 2 and all even rnds: Purl.

Continue working in garter stitch until both sections of the muff are the same length.

BO kwise.

Assembly

Fold the muff so that the CO and BO edges are together and the knit side of the alpaca section is facing out. Pin in place along the open edge of the muff. Thread a tapestry needle with yarn A, and sew the two edges together.

Finishing

Weave in all ends.

Felting

Turn the muff so that the yarn A side is facing out. Felt the muff in the washing machine as directed in the "Special Techniques" section. Once the muff is the desired size, pull it into shape and block it by stuffing it with plastic bags so that it maintains a cylindrical shape. Air dry the felted side then turn the muff inside out to air dry the furry side. Once dry, the fur can be fluffed up by hand or with a soft brush.

Red Riding Hood

As she skips off to Grandmother's house with her basket of goodies, there can be no mistaking Little Red Riding Hood. She is certainly one of the most famous and beloved of all fairy tale characters. In this design a subtle lace pattern, garter stitch hood, and decorative closures bring the fairy tale to life. Warm and stylish, this striking cape makes an enchanting addition to any young girl's wardrobe.

Cape

This cozy wrap is worked in one piece from the bottom up. Once the body of the cape is completed, stitches are decreased to form the yoke. The hood is worked from the neckline edge up and is finished off with a three-needle bind-off.

SIZES

12–24 months (2–4 years, 6–8 years)

FINISHED MEASUREMENTS

Length from front neckline edge to lower edge of front band:
    17 (20, 23^1/$_2$)" [42 (51, 60)cm]
Width at lower edge for all sizes: 45" (114cm)

Sample size 6–8 years

MATERIALS

Plymouth *Suri Merino* (55% suri alpaca, 45% extra -fine merino;
    110 yd. [100m] per 50g skein): #2055 Red, 8 (9, 10) skeins
US 5 (3.75mm) 24" circular needle
US 5 (3.75mm) 16" circular needle
US 6 (4mm) 24" circular needle
US 6 (4mm) 32" circular needle
15 stitch markers
Row counter
Tapestry needle
2 metal clasps
Sewing needle
Sewing thread to match yarn
24" (61cm) of ^{5}/$_8$" (16mm) ribbon (optional)

GAUGE

19 sts and 34 rows = 4" (10cm) in garter stitch on US 6 (4mm)
    needle, or size needed to obtain gauge

STITCH PATTERNS

Garter stitch worked flat—Knit all stitches every row.
K2tog (page 149)
Sk2po (page 151)
M1L (page 149)
M1R (page 149)
Yo (page 148)

SPECIAL TECHNIQUES

Three-needle bind-off (page 151)

Instructions

Cape

With 32" US 6 needle, CO 209 sts.

NOTE: The body of the cape is made up of a 12-row patt. There are 14 sts in each repeat. The patt is rep 14 times across the body of the cape and is bordered by a 6-stitch garter placket at the left and right fronts. An extra stitch is included at the left front edge to center the stitch patt. The Preparatory Row is worked only once.

Preparatory Row (RS): K6, pm, *k14, pm; rep from * 13 times, end k1, pm, k6.
Row 1 (WS): K6, sm, k1, sm, *yo, k5, sk2po, k5, yo, k1, sm; rep from * across row, end k6.
Row 2 and all even rows (RS): Knit, slipping markers as you go.
Row 3: K6, sm, k1, sm, *k1, yo, k4, sk2po, k4, yo, k2, sm; rep from * across row, end k6.
Row 5: K6, sm, k1, sm, *k2, yo, k3, sk2po, k3, yo, k3, sm; rep from * across row, end k6.
Row 7: K6, sm, k1, sm, *k3, yo, k2, sk2po, k2, yo, k4, sm; rep from * across row, end k6.
Row 9: K6, sm, k1, sm, *k4, yo, k1, sk2po, k1, yo, k5, sm; rep from * across row, end k6.
Row 11: K6, sm, k1, sm, *k5, yo, sk2po, yo, k6, sm; rep from * across row, end k6.
Row 12: Knit.

Rep Rows 1–12 of patt 6 (8, 10) times total, ending with a RS row.

Yoke Shaping

The yoke is worked in garter stitch. Three dec rows shape the yoke and neckline.

Rows 1–4: Knit, discarding all but the first and last markers.
Row 5 (WS): K6, sm, *k2tog, k1; rep from * to last 2 sts before last marker, k2tog, sm, k6—143 sts.
Rows 6–18: Knit.
Row 19 (WS): K6, sm, *k2tog, k1; rep from * to last 2 sts before last marker, k2tog, sm, k6—99 sts.

Rows 20–30: Knit.
Row 31 (WS): K6, sm, *k2tog, k1; rep from * across row, sm, k6—70 sts.
Rows 32–48: Knit.
Row 49 (WS): K6, sm, BO all stitches to next marker, sm, k6. Do not cut yarn.

Hood

Switch to 24" US 5 needle.

In the next row, you will pick up and knit into the stitches that you just bound off. While it may seem odd to BO stitches and immediately pick them up again, the purpose of this step is to strengthen the neckline edge and prevent stretching. If you do not wish to BO and pick up stitches, the same end result can be accomplished by knitting this row with the US 5 needle, proceeding to Row 1 of the hood section, and then sewing a ribbon facing along the inside neckline edge after the knitting is complete.

Row 1 (RS): K6, pick up 58 sts (1 for each stitch that you CO in the previous row), k6—70 sts.
Row 2 (WS): K35, pm, k35.
Rows 3–6: Knit, slipping marker.
Row 7 (RS): Knit to within 1 st of marker, M1R, k1, sm, k1, M1L, k to end—72 sts.
Row 8: Knit.
Rows 9–16: Rep Rows 7 and 8—80 sts.

Knit remainder of hood in garter stitch without further shaping until hood measures 9 (10, 12)" [23 (25, 30)cm] from the pick up row, ending with a RS row.

Hood Seam
The hood seam runs along the top of the head from the front to the back.

Slip the first 40 sts onto 16" US 5 needle. Fold hood in half so that the RS face each other and the front edges of the hood line up together. With WS facing, work a three-needle bind-off, beg at the front edge and working toward the fold at the back of the hood. Cut yarn and fasten off rem stitch.

Finishing

Weave in all ends. Block cape.

If desired, sew a ribbon facing to the inside edge of the right and left front yoke. This step is optional, but it does add durability to the front edges of the yoke (see page 159 for facing instructions).

Pin the clasps to the front edges of the cape yoke—the first one about level with the pick-up row where the hood begins, and the second just above the beginning of the garter stitch yoke. Sew clasps in place.

Hansel and Gretel

ost and alone, Hansel and Gretel bravely wander through the forest, trailing breadcrumbs, feasting upon a gingerbread house and cleverly outwitting troublesome grown-ups. Theirs is a story of real childhood adventure.

I have always loved this resourceful brother and sister team. I remember looking at an illustration of them in a favorite collection of fairy tales when I was a child. The woods in the picture were dark and foreboding and at the end of the path you could just glimpse a gingerbread house illuminated by a sunbeam. The illustrations had a rustic, Old World feel that I found utterly charming. That collection of fairy tales is long gone, but I can still clearly see Hansel and Gretel huddled together in the forest, and even now can recall the embroidery on Gretel's frock and Hansel's waistcoat.

This sweater and jumper are an updated version of what Hansel and Gretel might wear on their woodland trek. Made in warm fall colors, these designs were inspired by traditional European folk art. Soft washable wool and simple shaping make these outfits perfect for days of play and afternoon walks in the woods.

Sweater

This design is worked flat, from the bottom up, with simple shaping and seamless construction. The fronts and back are knitted as one piece with a decorative Fair Isle border. At the armholes, the piece is divided for the fronts and the back. After the body is finished and the shoulder seams are complete, stitches are picked up around the armhole edge and the sleeves are worked in the round to the cuff. Garter stitch front bands and decorative clasps complete the traditional look of this sweater.

SIZES

6–12 months (2 years, 4 years, 6 years)

FINISHED MEASUREMENTS

Chest: 22 (26, 28, 30)" [56 (66, 71, 76)cm]
Shoulder to hem: 12¹/₂ (14, 15¹/₂, 17)" [32 (36, 39, 43)cm]

Sample size 6 years

MATERIALS

Cascade Yarns *220 Superwash* (100% superwash wool; 220 yd. [201m] per 100g skein): #819 Truffle (color A), 2 (3, 3, 3) skeins; #891 Olive (color B), 1 skein; #822 Orange (color C), 1 skein
US 4 (3.5mm) 16" circular needle
US 4 (3.5mm) 24" circular needle
US 4 (3.5mm) double-pointed needles
US 6 (4 mm) 16" circular needle
US 6 (4 mm) 24" circular needle
US 6 (4 mm) double-pointed needles
Row counter
Stitch markers
Tapestry needle
4 metal clasps
Sewing needle
Sewing thread to match yarn
1 yd. (1m) of ⁵/₈" (18mm) ribbon (optional)

GAUGE

20 sts and 26 rows = 4" (10cm) in St st on US 6 (4mm) needle, or size needed to obtain gauge

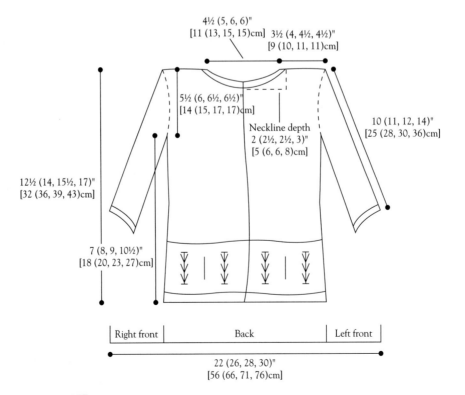

STITCH PATTERNS

Stockinette stitch worked flat—Knit on RS rows; purl on WS rows.
Stockinette stitch worked in the round—Knit all stitches every round.
Garter stitch worked flat—Knit all stitches every row.
Garter stitch worked in the round—Knit a round, purl a round.
K2tog (page 149)
P2tog tbl (page 150)
Ssk (page 150)

SPECIAL TECHNIQUES
Three-needle bind-off (page 151)
Fair Isle colorwork (page 157)

Instructions

Sweater Border and Body

With 24" US 4 needle and color A, CO 111 (129, 141, 149) sts.

Rows 1–6: Knit.
Change to 24" US 6 needle and color B.
Row 7 (RS): Knit.
Row 8: Knit.
Rows 9 and 10: Knit color C.
Row 11: Knit color A.
Row 12: Purl color B.

Pattern Band

The colorwork in this section is worked in Fair Isle. When working Fair Isle, you should always bring the new color *under* the one last used. This creates a twist, locking the yarn in place and preventing unwanted holes at the color changes.

Read the patt chart on the next page from the bottom up, from right to left on RS (odd numbered) rows and from left to right on WS (even numbered) rows.

NOTE: For the two smaller sizes, use the 16-row patt chart and for the two larger sizes, use the 22-row patt chart.

Row 1 (RS): K2 (2, 1, 3) color A, pm, *k1 (1, 2, 1) color A, work Row 1 of chart over next 15 sts, using color A as the background and color B as the patt motif, k1 (1, 2, 1) color A, k1 color B, pm; rep from * 4 (5, 5, 6) times, end k1 (1, 2, 1) color A, work row 1 of chart over next 15 sts, k1 (1, 2, 1) color A, pm, k2 (2, 1, 3) color A.
Row 2 (WS): P2 (2, 1, 3) color A, sm, p1 (1, 2, 1) color A, work Row 2 of chart over next 15 sts, p1 (1, 2, 1) color A, *sm, p1 color B, p1 (1, 2, 1) color A, work Row 2 of chart over next 15 sts, p1 (1, 2, 1) color A; rep from * 4 (5, 5, 6) times, end sm, p2 (2, 1, 3) color A.
Continue working Fair Isle patt in St st as established until all rows of chart have been worked.
Next row (RS): Knit color A.
Next row (WS): Purl color A.

To finish the pattern band knit two rows color C and then knit two rows color B. Cut colors B and C.

Chart for Sizes 6 Months–2 Years

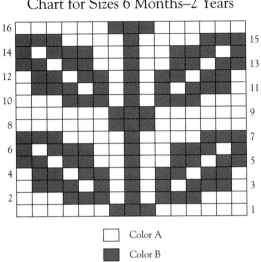

☐ Color A
■ Color B

Chart for Sizes 4–6 Years

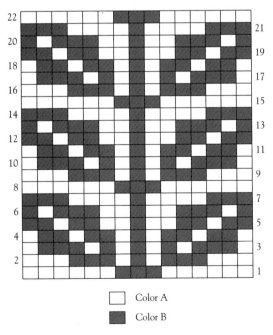

☐ Color A
■ Color B

The remainder of the sweater body is worked in St st with color A only. Continue until piece measures 7 (8, 9, 10½)" [18 (20, 23, 27) cm] from CO edge, ending with a WS row.

Divide for Fronts and Back

Right Front
Use the 16" US 6 needle to work the right front.

Next row (RS): K27 (31, 34, 36) sts for right front. Turn work, leaving rem 84 (98, 107, 113) sts on 24" needle to be worked later for the sweater back and left front.
Next row (WS): Beg at the right armhole, p27 (31, 34, 36) to center opening.

Continue to work in St st on right front stitches only until the piece measures 10 (11½, 13, 14)" [25 (29, 33, 36)cm] from CO edge, ending with a WS row.

Right Neckline Shaping
Row 1 (RS): BO 4 (5, 6, 6) at right front neck edge, k to end—23 (26, 28, 30) sts.
Row 2: Purl to last 2 sts, p2tog tbl—22 (25, 27, 29) sts.
Row 3: Ssk, k to end—21 (24, 26, 28) sts.
Rows 4 and 5: Rep Rows 2 and 3—19 (22, 24, 26) sts.
Row 6 (WS): Purl.
Row 7: Ssk, k to end—18 (21, 23, 25) sts.
Rem rows: Rep last two rows 1 (1, 2, 2) time(s)—17 (20, 21, 23) sts.

Continue in St st without further shaping until right front measures 12½ (14, 15½, 17)" [32 (36, 39, 43)cm] from CO edge, ending with a WS row.

Cut yarn, leaving a long tail, and put right shoulder stitches on a holder for later.

Sweater Back
With RS facing and using 16" US 6 needle, join color A at right armhole and k57 (67, 73, 77) sts for the sweater back. Turn work, leaving the rem 27 (31, 34, 36) sts for left front on the 24" needle to be worked later.

Beg at left armhole with WS facing, work in St st until back measures 12½ (14, 15½, 17)" [32 (36, 39, 43)cm] from CO edge, ending with a WS row. Cut yarn, leaving rem stitches on 16" needle.

Left Front

With RS facing, join yarn A at left armhole and knit across the 27 (31, 34, 36) sts on hold for the left front. Work as for right front until left front measures 10 (11½, 13, 14)" [25 (29, 33, 36)cm] from CO edge, ending with a RS row.

Left Neckline Shaping

Row 1 (WS): BO 4 (5, 6, 6) sts at left neck edge, p to end—23 (26, 28, 30) sts.

Row 2 (RS): Beg at left armhole, k to last 2 sts, k2tog—22 (25, 27, 29) sts.

Row 3: P2tog, p to end—21 (24, 26, 28) sts.

Rows 4 and 5: Rep Rows 2 and 3—19 (22, 24, 26) sts.

Row 6 (RS): K to last 2 sts, k2tog—18 (21, 23, 25) sts.

Row 7: Purl.

Rem rows: Rep last two rows 1 (1, 2, 2) time(s)—17 (20, 21, 23) sts.

Continue in St st without further shaping until front measures 12½ (14, 15½, 17)" [32 (36, 39, 43)cm], ending with a WS row. Do not cut yarn.

Shoulder Seams

Put the right and left front shoulder stitches each on a US 4 dpn. The stitches for the sweater back rem on the 16" needle.

With RS of work together, and the back of the sweater facing you, begin working at the left armhole edge. Using a US 4 dpn or the 24" needle, work a three-needle bind-off across 17 (20, 21, 23) sts for the left shoulder. BO center 23 (27, 31, 31) sts pwise for the back of the neck and then work three-needle bind-off across the rem 17 (20, 21, 23) sts for the right shoulder. Cut yarn and fasten off.

Sleeves

The sleeve stitches are picked up along the armhole edge and worked in the round.

Beg at one of the underarms with RS facing and using the US 4 dpns and color A, pick up 56 (60, 66, 72) sts around the armhole edge, and place a marker. Arrange the stitches evenly on the dpns. Join in the round.

Rnd 1: Knit.
Switch to the US 6 dpns.

Rnds 2–4: Knit.

Rnd 5: K1, ssk, k to within 3 sts of marker, k2tog, k1 (2 sts dec)—54 (58, 64, 70) sts.

Rep last 4 rounds, dec 2 sts as established every fourth round 9 (9, 10, 10) times to 36 (40, 44, 50) sts. From here, dec 2 sts as established every sixth round 2 (3, 4, 5) times—32 (34, 36, 40) sts.

Knit without shaping until sleeve measures 9 (10, 11, 13)" [23 (25, 28, 33)cm].

Cuff

Switch to US 4 dpns and color C.

Rnd 1: Knit.

Rnd 2: Purl.

Rnd 3: Knit color B.

Rnd 4: Purl color B.

Rnds 5, 7, and 9: Knit color A.
Rnds 6, 8, and 10: Purl color A.
BO pwise in color A.

Repeat for second sleeve.

Front Bands

With RS facing and using 24" US 4 needle and color A, pick up 52 (60, 67, 75) sts evenly along one side of the sweater front opening. Knit 6 rows. BO kwise.

Rep for opposite front.

Neck Band

With RS facing, 16" US 4 needle, and color C, pick up 50 (56, 62, 68) sts evenly around the neckline beginning at the neck edge of the right front band and ending at the neck edge of the left front band.

Row 1 (WS): Knit.
Rows 2 and 3: Knit color B.
Rows 4–10: Knit color A.
BO kwise.

Finishing

Weave in all loose ends. Block sweater. Reinforce front bands by sewing ribbon facing to WS of the bands (optional). Position the metal clasps evenly spaced along front bands and sew into place.

Jumper

This jumper is worked in the round from the bottom up. The hem is embellished with bobbles, ridges of reverse stockinette stitch, and a floral band. All are worked directly into the pattern and require no sewing after the jumper is complete. The flower band is a slip stitch pattern.

It creates the look of embroidery by elongating stitches for the leaves and stem. It is fun to work and, like most slip stitch patterns, uses only one color per row. The rest of this piece is knitted in stockinette stitch. Stitches are decreased for the bodice, which is worked in the round up to the armholes and in rows from the armhole edge up to the shoulder seams. Crochet picot edging and chain stitch trim the neckline and armholes.

SIZES

6–12 months (2 years, 4 years, 6 years)

FINISHED MEASUREMENTS

Chest: 20 (22, 24, 26)" [51 (56, 61, 66)cm]
Length from shoulder to hem: 16$\frac{1}{2}$ (19$\frac{1}{2}$, 22$\frac{1}{2}$, 26)" [42 (50, 57, 66)cm]

Sample size 4 years

MATERIALS

Cascade Yarns *220 Superwash* (100% superwash wool; 220 yd. [201m] per 100g skein): #819 Truffle (color A), 3 (4, 4, 5) skeins; #822 Orange (color B), 1 skein; #839 Pink (color C), 1 skein; #891 Olive (color D), 1 skein
US 6 (4mm) 16" circular needle
US 6 (4mm) 24" circular needle
US 7 (4.5mm) 16" circular needle
US 7 (4.5mm) 24" circular needle
US size G (4mm) crochet hook
Row counter
Stitch markers
Tapestry needle

GAUGE

Skirt: 18 sts and 24 rows = 4" (10cm) in St st on US 7 (4.5mm) needle, or size needed to obtain gauge
Bodice: 20 sts and 26 rows = 4" (10cm) in St st on US 6 (4mm) needle, or size needed to obtain gauge

STITCH PATTERNS

Stockinette stitch worked in the round—Knit all stitches every round.
Stockinette stitch worked flat—Knit on RS rows; purl on WS rows.
Reverse stockinette stitch worked in the round—Purl all stitches every round.
MB (make bobble)—*(P3 in the next stitch, turn, k3, turn, sl 1, k2tog, psso); rep from *.
K2tog (page 149)
Ssk (page 150)
Yo (page 148)

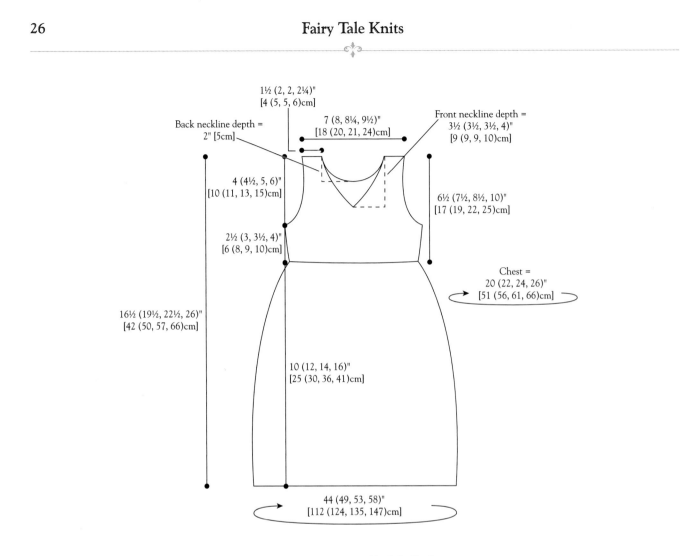

SPECIAL TECHNIQUES

Three-needle bind-off (page 151)
Crochet picot trim (see instructions in this pattern)
Crochet chain stitch edging (see instructions in this pattern)

Instructions

Jumper Border

With 24" US 6 needle and color B, CO 200 (220, 240, 260) sts, pm and join in the round.

Rnd 1: Purl.
Rnd 2: *P9, (k1, yo, k1, yo, k1) in the next stitch, turn, k5, turn, p5, pass second, third, fourth, and fifth stitches over the first stitch; rep from * to end. Do not cut yarn. Switch to 24" US 7 needle for the remainder of the skirt.

Rnd 3: Purl.
Rnd 4: Join color C and knit.
Rnds 5 and 6: Purl color C. Cut yarn.
Rnd 7: Knit color B.
Rnds 8 and 9: Purl color B. Cut yarn.
Rnds 10–13: Join color A and knit. Do not cut yarn.
Rnd 14: Join color D and knit. Do not cut yarn.

Flower Band Stitch Pattern

In this stitch pattern, stems are formed for each flower from elongated stitches. You will create these long vertical stitches by winding extra wraps around the working needle (RH needle) in Rnd 1. On subsequent rounds, the stitch is slipped with the yarn at the back of the work. On Rnd 6, you will rearrange the stitches so that the stems branch out. Bobbles are worked above each stem stitch to create the flowers.

Rnd 1: Still using color D, p3, *p3 wrapping the working yarn around the RH needle 3 times for each stitch, p7; rep from * to last 7 sts, end p3 wrapping yarn 3 times for each stitch, p4. Cut color D.

Switch to color A.
Rnd 2: K3, *sl 3 wyib dropping the extra wraps, k3, sl 1 wyib, k3; rep from * to last 7 sts, end sl 3 wyib dropping extra wraps, k3, sl 1 wyib.
Rnds 3, 4, and 5: K3, *sl 3 wyib, k7; rep from * to last 7 sts, end sl 3 wyib, k4.
Rnd 6: K1, *sl 2 background sts wyib, drop first leaf stitch off LH needle (at front of work), place the 2 background sts back onto the LH needle, then pick up the dropped leaf stitch with the tip of the LH needle and knit it, knit the 2 background sts slipped previously, knit the second leaf stitch, drop the third leaf stitch off the LH needle, knit the next 2 background sts, place the dropped leaf stitch back on the LH needle and knit it, k3; rep from * until 9 sts rem. Work last 9 sts by rep the patt as established, ending with k2 instead of k3.

Change to color C.
Rnd 7: *Sl 1 wyib, [(k1, p1, k1) in next stitch, sl 2 wyib] 3 times; rep from * to end.
Rnd 8: *Sl 1 wyib, (MB, sl 2 wyib) 3 times; rep from * to end.

Change to color A.
Rnd 9: *K1, (k1 tbl, k2) 3 times; rep from * to end.
Rem skirt rnds: Knit every round (St st) until skirt measures 10 (12, 14, 16)" [25 (30, 36, 41)cm] from CO edge.

Waistline Shaping
Switch to US 6 needle for the remainder of the bodice. You will use the 16" needle for the two smaller sizes and the 24" needle for the two largest sizes.

With color B, *k0 (1, 0, 1), k2tog 25 (27, 30, 32) times; rep from * 3 times to end—100 (112, 120, 132) sts.

Next rnd: Still using color B, purl.

Bodice
Use color A for the remainder of the bodice.

Knit every round until the jumper measures 12½ (15, 17½, 20)" [32 (38, 44, 51)cm] from CO edge.

Divide for Front and Back
The bodice will be worked back and forth in rows after dividing the stitches for front and back.

Back Armhole Shaping
Row 1 (RS): BO 4 sts for right armhole edge, knit until there are 46 (52, 56, 62) sts on the RH needle, turn.
Put rem 50 (56, 60, 66) sts on a holder for the bodice front to be worked later.
Row 2 (WS): BO 4 sts for left armhole edge, p to end of row—42 (48, 52, 58) sts.
Row 3: Ssk, k to last 2 sts, k2tog—40 (46, 50, 56) sts.
Row 4: Purl.
Rep last two rows 2 (3, 4, 4) times—36 (40, 42, 48) sts.

Continue to work St st until armhole measures 2½ (3, 3½, 3½)" [6 (8, 9, 9)cm], ending with a WS row.

Back Neckline Shaping
The shaping for the right and left back shoulder straps is worked simultaneously. After working across the stitches for the right shoulder, a second skein of yarn is introduced for the back of the neck and the left shoulder. On each row you will work one shoulder with one skein, and the other shoulder with the second skein. You can choose to work the shoulders on two separate needles or use the same circular for both shoulders.

Row 1 (RS): K11 (13, 14, 16) sts for right shoulder strap. Join a second skein of yarn, BO center 14 (14, 14, 16) sts for the center back of the neck, k11 (13, 14, 16) sts rem for left shoulder strap.

Row 2 and all even rows: Purl across each shoulder strap.

Row 3: K9 (11, 12, 14), k2tog at right neck edge, move to left strap, ssk at left neck edge, k9 (11, 12, 14)—10 (12, 13, 15) sts rem for each shoulder.

Rep last two rows 2 (2, 3, 3) times—8 (10, 10, 12) sts.

Continue without further shaping until armhole measures 4½ (5, 5½, 6)" [11 (13, 14, 15)cm], ending with a WS row. Put shoulder stitches on holders. Cut yarn, leaving a long tail.

Front Armhole Shaping

Slide the stitches on reserve for the bodice front onto either the 16" or 24" US 6 needle.

With RS facing and beg at left underarm, join yarn A and work front bodice armhole shaping as for back to 36 (40, 42, 48) sts. Begin front neckline shaping when the armhole measures 1 (1½, 2, 2)" [3 (4, 5, 5)cm], ending with a WS row.

Front Neckline Shaping

Work the front neckline as a V-neck, joining second skein of yarn and working both sides of the neckline simultaneously, as you did for the back.

Row 1 (RS): K16 (18, 19, 22), k2tog at left neck edge. Join a second skein of yarn for the right front. Ssk at right front neck edge, k16 (18, 19, 22)—17 (19, 20, 23) sts rem for each shoulder.

Row 2: Purl.

Row 3: K15 (17, 18, 21), k2tog, move to right front, ssk, k15 (17, 18, 21)—16 (18, 19, 22) sts rem for each shoulder.

Rep last two rows until 8 (10, 10, 12) sts rem for each shoulder. Continue to work St st without further shaping until armhole measures 4½ (5, 5½, 6)" [11 (13, 14, 15)cm], ending with a purl row.

Shoulder Seams

Slide the stitches of the front and back left shoulder onto two separate US 6 dpns. Turn the jumper inside out so that the RS are together. Beg at the left armhole edge with the back of the jumper and WS of work facing. Hold the dpns parallel to one another, join color A and work a three-needle bind-off to form the left shoulder seam. Cut yarn and fasten off.

Slide the stitches for the right shoulder onto dpns as for left shoulder. Arrange work so that the front of the jumper is facing you. Beg at the armhole, join yarn and rep for right shoulder seam.

Neckline and Armhole Trim

Weave in all loose ends before beg neckline and armhole trim.

Crochet picot trim and crochet chain stitch edging embellish the armholes and the neckline of the bodice. For the armhole you will begin and end both the picot trim and chain stitch edging at the underarm, and for the neckline you will begin and end at the center of the V-neck shaping. Because the trim is worked the same way for the neckline and both armholes, it doesn't matter which one you work first.

Crochet Picot Trim

The crochet picot trim is worked along the edge stitches of the armhole and neck openings. To do this, you will work into the edge stitches of these openings.

With RS facing, crochet hook, and color B, crochet into an edge stitch at the center of the V-neck or at the underarm of one of the armholes. To do this, hold the working yarn at the back (WS) of work and insert the hook from the RS of the work to the WS. Wrap a loop around the hook and pull the loop up through the bodice fabric to the RS of work. You now have a loop around the crochet hook on the RS of work.

*Chain 3 sts, insert the hook back into the original stitch and slip stitch (bring the first loop over the last chain loop without wrapping yarn around hook). Single crochet 2 sts, slip stitch and rep from * around.

When you are back at your starting place, cut yarn and fasten off end. See page 158 for crochet diagrams and instructions.

Crochet Chain Stitch Edging

This crochet edging is worked through the knitted fabric and mimics embroidered chain stitch.

After the crochet picot trim is complete, you will crochet a chain through the bodice fabric along the base of the picot trim with color C. *Hold the yarn at the back (WS) of work and insert the crochet hook into the front (RS) of the work to bring a loop up to the knit side of the fabric as previously explained. Move to the next stitch, insert hook into the bodice as before, wrap yarn around hook and pull hook back up to the RS. Pull the second loop through the first loop of the hook. Rep from *. When you have chained your way back to the starting point, work 1 last stitch into the stitch worked at the beg. Cut yarn and thread tail through a tapestry needle. Pull the yarn to the WS of work, fasten off, and weave in ends.

Finishing

Weave in ends. Block piece.

Cinderella

orking around the castle by day and dancing with Prince Charming by night .... Cinderella is one busy girl. This fairy-tale princess needs a dress that will work around the clock. Designed to go from preschool to party, this dress, sash, and apron ensemble is sure to delight any Cinderella wannabe.

Dress with Sash

Eyelet trim and ribbons combine with simple shaping to make a dress that's pretty and comfy enough to wear all day. Everything about this dress, from the delicate, lacy details to the sheen of the cotton yarn and ribbons, is fresh, soft and altogether girly. A ribbon sash, adorned with a bouquet of knitted flowers, adds to the charm of this sweet outfit. Pair this dress with the flower sash for dress-up or with the apron for a day around the castle. Either way, your little girl with feel great and look adorable.

Apron

Tidying up is bound to be more fun with this lacy apron. It looks darling with the Cinderella dress, and with skirts and jeans as well. Chances are that your little girl with want to wear it with everything she owns. Perfect for wearing at home or about town, this apron is an accessory that will please the Cinderella in your castle.

Dress with Sash

This dress is worked in one piece from the hem up. The skirt is worked in the round to the lower bodice edge. Stitches are decreased for the bodice, and the work is divided for the bodice fronts and back. The bodice is knitted flat in stockinette stitch up to the shoulders. A three-needle bind-off joins the shoulder seams. Sleeve stitches are picked up from the armhole edge, and the sleeves are knit in the round from the armhole edge down to the cuff.

SIZES

1–2 years (3–4 years, 5–6 years)

FINISHED MEASUREMENTS

Chest: 22 (24, 26)" [56 (61, 66)cm]
Length from hem to shoulder: 20¹/₂ (24, 27¹/₂)" [52 (61, 70)cm]

Sample sizes 3–4 years/Hydrangea and 1–2 years/Butter

MATERIALS

Knit Picks *Shine Sport* (60% pima cotton, 40% modal; 110 yd. [100.6m] per 50g skein): Color #8056 Hydrangea or #6567 Butter, 6 (9, 10) skeins; #6566 Violet, 1 skein (for flowers)
US 4 (3.5mm) 16" circular needle
US 4 (3.5mm) 24" circular needle
US 4 (3.5mm) double-pointed needles
US 3 (3.25mm) 16" circular needle
US 3 (3.25mm) 24" circular needle
US size F (3.75mm) crochet hook
Row counter
Stitch markers

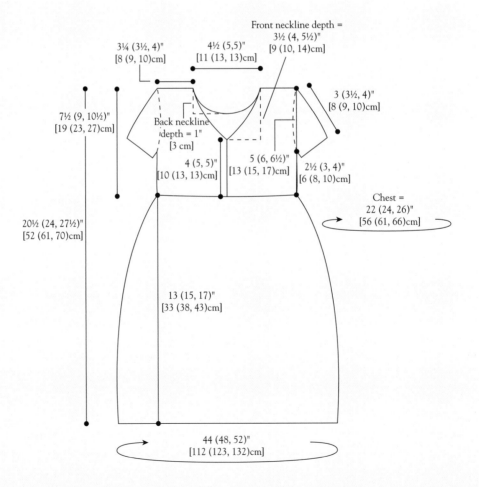

Front neckline depth =
3½ (4, 5½)"
[9 (10, 14)cm]

3¼ (3½, 4)"
[8 (9, 10)cm]

4½ (5,5)"
[11 (13, 13)cm]

3 (3½, 4)"
[8 (9, 10)cm]

7½ (9, 10½)"
[19 (23, 27)cm]

Back neckline
depth = 1"
[3 cm]

4 (5, 5)"
[10 (13, 13)cm]

5 (6, 6½)"
[13 (15, 17)cm]

2½ (3, 4)"
[6 (8, 10)cm]

Chest =
22 (24, 26)"
[56 (61, 66)cm]

20½ (24, 27½)"
[52 (61, 70)cm]

13 (15, 17)"
[33 (38, 43)cm]

44 (48, 52)"
[112 (123, 132)cm]

2 safety pins
Tapestry needle
Sewing needle
Sewing thread to match dress
$^3/_8$" (.95cm) buttons—4 to 5
2 yd. (2m) of 1$^1/_2$" (4cm) ribbon
1 yd. (1m) of $^1/_4$" (.64cm) ribbon

GAUGE

22 sts and 30 rows = 4" (10cm) in St st using US 4 (3.5mm) needles,
   or size needed to obtain gauge

STITCH PATTERNS

Stockinette stitch worked in the round—Knit all stitches every
   round.
Stockinette stitch worked flat—Knit on RS rows; purl on WS rows.
K2tog (page 149)
Ssk (page 150)
Kfb (page 148)
Yo (page 148)

SPECIAL TECHNIQUES

Crochet chain stitch (page 158)
Three-needle bind-off (page 151)
Bobbles (see instructions in this pattern)
Knitted flowers (see instructions in this pattern)

Instructions
Skirt

With 24" US 4 needle, CO 240 (264, 288) sts, placing a
marker at the end of the row.

Eyelet Band

Join work in a round, taking care not to twist stitches.

Rnd 1: Purl.
Rnd 2: Knit.
Rnd 3: Purl.
Rnd 4: *K2tog, yo; rep from * to marker.
Rnds 5 and 7: Purl.
Rnd 6: Knit.
Rnds 8–13: Knit.
Rnds 14–20: Rep rnds 1–7.
Rnds 21–26: Knit.
Rnds 27–33: Rep rnds 1–7.

From here, work in St st until skirt measures 13 (15, 17)"
[33 (38, 43)cm] from CO row.

Gather Skirt

*K2tog; rep from * to marker—120 (132, 144) sts.

Bodice

In the next round, you will bind-off stitches for the center
front of the dress and place a contrasting marker to indicate
the right underarm "seam." The original marker stays in
place to mark the left underarm.

K28 (31, 34) sts for the left front, BO 4 sts for the center
front. Do not cut yarn or fasten off the last stitch. K27 (30,
33) sts for the right front (you will have a total of 56 [62,
68] sts on the right needle), place contrasting marker for
the right underarm, k to end—116 (128, 140) sts. Cut yarn.

NOTE: From this point to the beg of the armholes, the bodice is worked back and forth in rows beg and ending at the center front opening. Begin all RS rows at right center front. Slip the markers at the underarms as you come to them.

With RS facing, join yarn at the right center front opening. Beg with a knit row, work back and forth in St st for 2½ (3, 4)" [6 (8, 10)cm], ending with a WS row.

Divide for Fronts and Back

Right Front

With 16" US 4 needle, RS facing and beg at the edge of the right front center opening, k28 (31, 34) sts to the right underarm (contrasting marker), turn. Leave the stitches for the back and the left front on the 24" needle for later, and work on the 28 (31, 34) sts for right front only.

Next row (WS): Beg at right underarm, purl to center front opening.

Continue to work in St st until the right front measures 4 (5, 5)" [10 (13, 13)cm] from beg of bodice, ending with a WS row.

Right Front Neckline Shaping

Row 1 (RS): K1, ssk, k to armhole edge—27 (30, 33) sts. Place a safety pin at the neck edge of Row 1 to mark the beg of the neck shaping.
Row 2: Purl.

Rep last 2 rows, decreasing 1 st at the neck edge every RS row 9 (10, 11) more times—18 (20, 22) sts.

Work in St st without further shaping until armhole opening measures 5 (6, 6½)" [13 (15, 17)cm], ending with a WS row. Cut yarn.
Put rem 18 (20, 22) sts for right shoulder on a holder.

Back

With 16" US 4 needle, RS facing, and beg at the right underarm, knit across 60 (66, 72) sts for the bodice back, turn and leave rem 28 (31, 34) sts for the left front on the 24" needle for later.

Working on the back sts only, and beg with a purl row, work in St st until back measures 4 (5, 5½)" [10 (13, 14) cm] from base of the armhole edge, ending with a purl row.

Back Neckline Shaping

NOTE: Both sides of the back neck are worked at the same time, each with a separate ball of yarn.

Row 1 (RS): K17 (19, 21), k2tog, k1, sl the next 20 (22, 24) sts onto a holder for back neck, join a new skein of yarn to work left shoulder, k1, ssk, k17 (19, 21)—19 (21, 23) sts for each shoulder.
Row 2 (WS): P19 (21, 23) sts for left shoulder, drop yarn, skip center neck stitches on holder, pick up yarn for right shoulder and p to end—19 (21, 23) sts for each shoulder.
Row 3: K16 (18, 20), k2tog, k1, drop yarn, skip reserved neck stitches, pick up yarn for left side, k1, ssk, k16 (18, 20)—18 (20, 22) sts each side.

Continue to work on the right and left back shoulders without further shaping until the back armhole openings measure 5 (6, 6½)" [13 (15, 17)cm], ending with a WS row. Cut yarn and put the right and left shoulder stitches on two separate holders.

Left Front

With 16" US 4 needle, RS facing, and beg at the left underarm, join yarn and k28 (31, 34) sts to end of row (edge of the left front center opening).

Next row: Beg at center opening, p28 (31, 34) sts to the left armhole edge.

Work left front in St st as established until the left front measures 4 (5, 5)" [10 (13, 13)cm] from beg of bodice, ending with a WS row.

Left Front Neckline Shaping

Row 1 (RS): K25 (28, 31), k2tog, k1—27 (30, 33) sts. Place a safety pin at the neck edge of Row 1 to mark the beg of the neck shaping.
Row 2 (WS): Purl.

Rep last 2 rows, continuing to dec (as established in Row 1) at neck edge of every RS row, 9 (10, 11) more times—18 (20, 22) sts.

Work in St st without further shaping until the length of the armhole opening is 5 (6, 6½)" [13 (15, 17)cm] (the same length as the bodice back), ending with a WS row.

Cut yarn and put rem 18 (20, 22) sts for left front shoulder on a holder.

Shoulder Seams

Slide each set of shoulder stitches onto a separate US 3 dpn. Turn the dress inside out so that the RS of the dress are together. With WS facing join yarn at the beg of the right armhole edge. Work a three-needle bind-off, joining the front and back right shoulder stitches together. Cut yarn and fasten off.

Leave the stitches for the center of the neck on the holder to be worked later.

Rep for left shoulder seam, working from the armhole to the neck edge.

Sleeves

With US 3 dpns, RS facing, and beg at the center of the left underarm, pick up 50 (62, 68) sts evenly around armhole opening. Divide stitches as evenly as possible on three dpns, pm, and join in the round.

Rnd 1: Knit.
Switch to US 4 dpns.
Rnds 2 and 3: Knit.
Rnd 4: Ssk, k to last 2 sts, k2tog—48 (60, 66) sts.

Rep last 4 rows 3 (4, 5) more times—42 (52, 56) sts. Continue to work in St st without further shaping until sleeve measures 2 (2½, 3)" [5 (6, 8)cm].

Eyelet Trim

Rnds 1, 3, 5, and 7: Purl.
Rnds 2 and 6: Knit.
Rnd 4: *K2tog, yo; rep from * to end.
Rnd 8: BO pwise. Cut yarn.

Rep for right sleeve.

Button and Buttonhole Band

Slide the stitches on hold for the back of the neck onto a US 3 dpn.

With 24" US 3 needle and RS facing, beg at the base of the right front center opening, and pick up 23 (28, 28) sts along the edge of the right front to the safety pin marking the beg of neckline shaping. Remove the safety pin and pm. Continue around the right front neckline, picking up 21 (24, 33) sts evenly between the marker and the dpn holding the stitches for the back of the neck. Knit across the 20 (22, 24) sts on hold for the back of the neck. Work left neckline edge as for right neckline, picking up 21 (24, 33) sts between the back of the neck and the safety pin marking the left neckline shaping. Remove the safety pin and place a contrasting marker. Continue as for right front center opening, picking up 23 (28, 28) sts from the neckline shaping to the lower edge of the left bodice front—108 (126, 146) sts.

Rows 1–3: Knit.
Row 4 (RS): K4, *k2tog, yo; rep from * to contrasting marker at left front neckline. Knit to base of left front.
Rows 5–8: Knit.
Row 9 (WS): BO kwise.
Fasten off.

Belt Loops

With crochet hook and main color, chain 16 sts, fasten off. Rep for second belt loop. Sew the belt loops along the right and left sides of the lower bodice.

Flowers

Make three flowers in color of choice.

Using US 3 dpns, CO 3 sts.
Row 1 (RS): Kfb, k to end—4 sts.
Rows 2, 4, 6, and 8 (WS): K2, p to end.
Rows 3 and 5: Rep Row 1—6 sts at end of Row 5.
Row 7: BO 4 sts, kfb—3 sts.
Rem rows: Rep Rows 1–8 three times, rep Rows 1–6 once.

BO all stitches. Cut yarn, leaving a 12" (30cm) tail. Thread the tail onto a tapestry needle. Pull the needle through the edges of the garter stitch ridges along the straight edge of the flower. Pull the yarn taut, drawing the flower into a circle. Fasten off. Cut yarn and weave the tail into the back side of the flower.

Bobbles

Make a bobble for each flower center.

With US 4 dpns and yarn color of choice, CO 1 st. K in front, back, front, back, and front again of stitch—5 sts.

Work in St st for 3 rows. Do not turn work after the last row.

Use the empty dpn to lift the second, third, fourth, and fifth stitches (one at a time) over the first stitch—1 st.

Cut yarn, leaving a 12" (30cm) tail. Fasten off by threading the tail through the rem stitch.

Tie the tails from the CO and BO edges together to gather the bobble. Thread a tapestry needle with one of the tails and weave it into the bobble.

Center bobble on top of flower and sew into place with the rem bobble tail.

Finishing

Weave in all loose ends.

Layer the eyelet band (right front) on top of the garter stitch band (left front), and sew the base of the bands to center front of the skirt.

Sew buttons evenly along left front button band. Sew flowers to ribbon sash as desired.

Cut two 12" (30cm) lengths of ¼" (.64cm) ribbon, thread it through the eyelet trim on each sleeve, and tie ends in a bow.

Apron

This apron is knit in one piece, from the bottom up, beginning with the hem and ending with the waistband and casing. When the knitting is finished, the casing is folded over and stitched in place. A length of ribbon threaded through the casing forms the apron ties.

SIZES
One size fits all

FINISHED MEASUREMENTS
NOTE: Measurements taken after blocking.

Width at hem: 17" (43cm)
Width at waistband: 10½" (27cm)
Length from upper waistband fold to lower edge of hem: 11¾"
    (30cm)

MATERIALS
Knit Picks *Shine Sport* (60% pima cotton, 40% modal; 110 yd.
    [100.6m] per 50g skein): Color #6563 Cream, 2 skeins
US 4 (3.5mm) needles
US 6 (4mm) needles
Stitch markers
Row counter
Tapestry needle
Sewing needle
Sewing thread to match apron
2 yd. (1.8m) of 1½" (4cm) double-sided ribbon

GAUGE
21 sts and 26 rows = 4" (10cm) in St st using US 6 (4mm) needles, or
    size needed to obtain gauge

STITCH PATTERNS
Stockinette stitch worked flat—Knit on RS rows; purl on WS rows.
K2tog (page 149)
Yo (page 148)

Instructions
Apron Skirt
With US 6 needle, CO 81 sts.
Rows 1, 3, and 5 (RS): Purl.
Rows 2, 4, and 6: Knit.
Row 7 (RS): K2, pm, *k2tog, k3, yo, k1, yo, k3, k2tog; rep
from * to last 2 sts, pm, k2.
Row 8 (WS): K2, sm, p77, sm, k2.
Rows 9–68: Rep Rows 7 and 8.

Waistband and Facing
Row 1 (RS): K2, sm, *(k2tog, k1) 3 times, k2tog; rep from
* to marker, sm, k2—53 sts.
Change to US 4 needles.
Rows 2–13: Knit across, slipping markers as you go.
The rem rows make up the waistband facing.

Row 14 (WS): K2, sm, p49, sm, k2.
Row 15: Knit.
Rows 16–21: Rep Rows 14 and 15.
Row 22 (WS): Rep Row 14.
Row 23: BO kwise.

Finishing
To form the apron casing, fold waistband facing to the
wrong side of the apron and pin the BO edge to the lower
edge of the waistband (along the upper edge of the apron
skirt). With needle and thread, sew the facing to the
waistband along the BO edge. Do not sew the right and left
short sides of the casing.
Weave in all ends.

Block the apron to the measurements listed above, gently
stretching the lower edge out and down so that the
scalloped hem is nicely defined.

Thread the ribbon through the waistband casing and tack
it into place at the side openings.

Flower Fairies

airy godmothers, flower fairies, sprites and pixies ... children's stories are filled with fairy folk. Of all of these, flower fairies are amongst the most enchanting. Spring and summer are especially good times to admire the handiwork of these wee folk. During these colorful months it is easy to imagine flower fairies donning the new blooms of the season, frolicking in woodland meadows, and stopping to rest upon buttercup beds. Included in this section are two fairy offerings for greeting and celebrating the season—a sweater coat and cloche for spring and a blossom sundress for summer. Fanciful and fun, these adorable outfits are destined to become perennial favorites.

Spring Sweater Coat and Cloche

Adorned with climbing roses, leafy details, and loops of ivy edging, this sweet sweater coat and cloche are as soft and fresh as the spring. This set is comfortable and easy to wear, perfect for woodland walks and cool spring days spent playing at the park.

Sundress

Made in the bright colors of high summer, this blossom fairy dress looks just like a happy Gerber daisy. Knit in a cotton/linen blend, it is perfect for the busy, hard-playing days of the season. Pair it with shorts, capris, or a skirt for a really fun summer look or with a shirt and leggings or jeans for fall and winter. This fanciful frock is sure to delight fairies and pixies of all sorts.

Spring Sweater Coat

The petal-shaped peplum of this sweater coat is worked in sturdy, non-curling garter stitch from the bottom up, and is bordered by a row of garter stitch leaves. The leaves are made on a separate needle and are knitted to the peplum at the bodice edge. The bodice is worked seamlessly in stockinette stitch with minimal shaping. The drop-shoulder sleeves are knitted in the round from the armholes down. The front bands and shawl collar of this sweater are shaped with short rows and trimmed with sections of attached and unattached I-cord. Knitted flowers and leaves embellish the collar and complete the flower fairy theme.

SIZES
6–18 months (2–4 years, 4–6 years)

FINISHED MEASUREMENTS
Chest: 22 (25, 28)" [56 (64, 71)cm]
Bodice length from shoulder to peplum band: 11 (12½, 14)" [28 (32, 36)cm]

Sample size 2–4 years

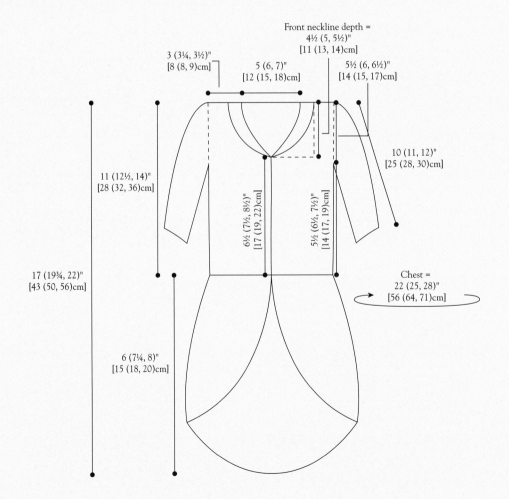

Front neckline depth =
4½ (5, 5½)"
[11 (13, 14)cm]

3 (3¼, 3½)"
[8 (8, 9)cm]

5 (6, 7)"
[12 (15, 18)cm]

5½ (6, 6½)"
[14 (15, 17)cm]

10 (11, 12)"
[25 (28, 30)cm]

11 (12½, 14)"
[28 (32, 36)cm]

6½ (7½, 8½)"
[17 (19, 22)cm]

5½ (6½, 7½)"
[14 (17, 19)cm]

17 (19¾, 22)"
[43 (50, 56)cm]

Chest =
22 (25, 28)"
[56 (64, 71)cm]

6 (7¼, 8)"
[15 (18, 20)cm]

MATERIALS

Knit Picks *Swish DK* (100% superwash wool; 123 yd. [112m] per 50g skein): #24051 Petal (color A), 5 (6, 8) skeins; #24058 Asparagus (color B), 2 skeins; #24052 Cornflower (color C), 1 skein; #24049 Eggplant (color D), 1 skein

US 5 (3.75mm) 16" circular needle

US 5 (3.75mm) 24" circular needle

US 5 (3.75mm) double-pointed needles

US 4 (3.5mm) 16" circular needle

US 4 (3.5mm) 24" circular needle

US 4 (3.5mm) double-pointed needles

2 safety pins

Stitch markers

Row counter

Stitch holder

Tapestry needle

³/₄" (2cm) buttons—3

GAUGE

22 sts and 28 rows = 4" (10cm) in St st on US 5 (3.75mm) needles, or size needed to obtain gauge

STITCH PATTERNS

Stockinette stitch worked flat—Knit on RS rows; purl on WS rows.

Stockinette stitch worked in the round—Knit all stitches every round.

Garter stitch worked flat—Knit all stitches every row.

I-cord (page 155)

W&t (page 154)

K2tog (page 149)

Sk2po (page 151)

Ssk (page 150)

Kfb (page 148)

M1L (page 149)

M1R (page 149)

Yo (page 148)

SPECIAL TECHNIQUES

Attached I-cord (see instructions in this pattern)

Short rows (page 154)

Three-needle bind-off (page 151)

Knitted flowers (see instructions in this pattern)

Knitted leaves (see instructions in this pattern)

Instructions

Peplum Band Leaves

Garter stitch leaves embellish the upper edge of the peplum. These leaves are knitted first, back and forth in rows. The peplum is worked on a separate needle. Once it is complete, the leaves are attached to the peplum and the work progresses to the bodice. There are nine leaves in all, five large and four small.

With color B and US 5 dpns, CO 1 st.

Row 1 (WS): K1, p1, k1 in the same stitch—3 sts.

Row 2: K1, pm, k1, pm, k1.

Row 3 and all odd rows through Row 11 (13, 15): K to marker, yo, sm, k1, sm, yo, k to end of row—13 (15, 17) sts.

Row 4 and all rem even rows (RS): Knit, slipping markers as you go.

For the 4 small leaves, knit an additional 4 rows beyond Row 11 (13, 15) without increasing. Discard markers as you work across the last row. Cut yarn, leaving a long tail.

For the 5 large leaves, knit an additional 10 rows beyond Row 11 (13, 15) without increasing. Discard markers as you work across the last row. Cut yarn, leaving a long tail.

Alternate making small and large leaves, beg and ending with a small leaf. Move the leaves to the 16" US 5 needle as they are completed, making sure that they are all facing the same direction—117 (135, 153) sts in all. Set aside.

Peplum

With 24" US 5 needle and color A, CO 68 (77, 88) sts.
Row 1 (WS): Sl 1, k rem stitches.
Row 2: K1, M1R, k to last stitch, M1L, k1—70 (79, 90) sts.
Row 3: Sl 1, M1R, k to last 2 sts, k1 tbl, M1L, k1—72 (81, 92) sts.
Rows 4–56 (65, 73): Rep Row 3—178 (205, 232) sts.
Row 57 (66, 74): Sl 1, k to last 2 sts, k1 tbl, k1.
Rows 58–60 (67–70, 75–78): Sl 1, k to end.

Gather Peplum (WS)
*K1, k2tog; rep from * to last stitch, k1—119 (137, 155) sts.

Join Leaves to Peplum

To join the leaves to the peplum, place the circular needle holding the leaves in front of the needle holding the peplum stitches. Hold the two needles parallel so that the RS of the leaves and the peplum are facing you, and the leaves are in front of the peplum. The working yarn should be trailing off the RH side of the peplum and each leaf.

With color B and 24" US 5 needles, knit the first stitch of the peplum as you would normally. Next, insert the RH needle into the first leaf stitch and the next peplum stitch kwise, and knit the 2 sts as one. Work across all of the leaf and peplum stitches, knitting them together. Move the tails of the leaves to the back of the work between the needles, weaving them in as you work across the row. End by knitting the rem peplum stitch.

Peplum Band

Continue working with color B for the peplum band.
Rows 1, 3, 5, and 7 (WS): Purl.
Rows 2, 4, and 6: Knit.

Row 8 (RS): To make the welt that forms the peplum band, each stitch in Row 7 is knitted together with its corresponding stitch from Row 1. With the tip of the left needle, reach to the back of the work and pick up the bar formed by the first stitch of Row 1. Knit this stitch together with the first stitch of Row 7 (the first live stitch on the LH needle). Continue in this manner across the row.
Row 9: Purl.
Cut yarn.

Bodice

Switch to color A for the rem of the bodice.

NOTE: For sizes 6–18 months and 4–6 years, 1 st is added by knitting into the front and back of a stitch at the middle of the row. This increase is omitted for the 2–4 years size. Because of this, you will knit across all stitches of Row 1 for size 2–4 years, without working the kfb increase.

Row 1 (RS): K58 (137, 77), kfb 1 (0, 1) time(s), k rem 60 (0, 77) sts—120 (137, 156) sts.
Row 2: Purl.

Work in St st until bodice measures 5½ (6½, 7½)" [14 (17, 19)cm] from beg of bodice, ending with a WS row.

Divide for Fronts and Back

With RS facing and using 16" US 5 needle, k30 (34, 39) for right front, turn. Use the 24" needle to hold rem stitches in reserve for sweater back and left front. These stitches will be worked later.

Right Front
Continue to work on these 30 (34, 39) sts in St st until bodice measures 6½, (7½, 8½) [17 (19, 22)cm] from peplum band, ending with a WS row.

Right Neckline Shaping
Row 1 (RS): K1, ssk, k to end—29 (33, 38) sts.
Place a safety pin at the neck edge of Row 1 to mark the beg of the neckline shaping. The safety pin will remain in place until you begin the front bands and collar of the sweater.
Row 2: Purl.
Rep last two rows decreasing at the neck edge every RS row 13 (15, 18) times—16 (18, 20) sts.

NOTE: Keep track of how many rows it takes to reach the following armhole measure, as it will be repeated on the left front.

Continue working in St st until the armhole edge measures 5½ (6, 6½)" [14 (15, 17)cm] from beg of armhole, and ending with a purl row. Cut yarn and put these 16 (18, 20) sts on a holder for later.

Back

With RS facing and using the 16" US 5 needle, join yarn at the base of the right armhole.

K across 60 (69, 78) sts, turn, and leave rem 30 (34, 39) sts for left front on the 24" needle for later.

Work on these 60 (69, 78) sts in St st until the back is the same length as the right front, ending with a purl row. Cut yarn and place stitches on a spare needle or holder for later.

Left Front

With RS facing and beg at the left armhole edge, join yarn and work across 30 (34, 39) sts in St st as for right front until left front measures 6½ (7½, 8½)" [16 (19, 22)cm] ending with a WS row.

Left Neckline Shaping

Work as for right front, reversing the neckline shaping as follows:
Row 1 (RS): K to last 3 sts, k2tog, k1—30 (36, 40) sts. Place a safety pin at the neck edge of Row 1 to mark the beg of the neckline shaping. The safety pin will remain in place until you begin the front bands and collar of the sweater.
Row 2: Purl.

Continue as established in Rows 1 and 2, decreasing at the neck edge every RS row until 16 (18, 20) sts rem and the left front measures same as right front and back, ending with a WS row.

Shoulder Seams

Place the 60 (69, 78) sts for back on 16" US 5 needle. Place stitches for right front on a US 5 dpn and rep for left front. Turn sweater inside out so that the RS of the sweater

are together. With the purl side of the sweater front facing you, and beg at the right armhole edge, join color A and work a three-needle bind-off across the 16 (18, 20) sts for the right shoulder. Cut yarn and fasten off.

Turn the work so that the back of the sweater is facing you and complete the left shoulder seam in the same manner, working from the armhole edge to the neck opening.

Put the rem stitches for the back of the neck on a holder for later.

Sleeves

With US 4 dpns, RS facing and beg at the base of the right armhole, join color A and pick up 60 (66, 70) sts evenly around the armhole edge. Arrange stitches evenly on dpns, pm, and join in the round.

Rnd 1: Knit.
Change to US 5 dpns.
Rnds 2 and 3: Knit.
Rnd 4: K1, ssk, k to last 3 sts, k2tog, k1—58 (64, 68) sts.
Rnds 5, 6, and 7: Knit.
Rep last four rounds 15 (17, 19) times—28 (30, 30) sts.

Continue without further shaping until the sleeve measures 9½ (10½, 11½)" [24 (27, 29)cm] from the shoulder down.

Cuff

Switch to US 4 dpns.
Rnds 1 and 3: Purl.
Rnds 2 and 4: Knit.
BO pwise.

Repeat for left sleeve.

Collar, Button Band, and Buttonhole Band

NOTE: The buttonhole band, collar, and button band are worked in one piece. Stitches are picked up for all of the above at the same time, beg with the stitches for the buttonhole band on the right front, moving up into the neckline for the collar, and then around to the button band stitches on the left front of the sweater. The same needle is used throughout.

With 24" US 4 needle and color A, RS facing, and beg at the bottom edge of the right front bodice, pick up 30 (36, 40) sts up to the safety pin marking the beg of the right neckline shaping, remove safety pin, pm, pick up 26 (28, 32) sts up right front neckline to shoulder seam, pm, k across the 28 (33, 38) sts on hold for the back neck, pm, pick up 26 (28, 32) sts down left front neckline to the safety pin marking the left neckline shaping, remove safety pin, pm, pick up 30 (36, 40) sts down to lower edge of left front bodice—140 (161, 182) sts total.

Button Band and Buttonhole Band
Rows 1–5: Knit.
Work buttonholes on right front bodice as follows.
Row 6 (RS): K3, k2tog, yo twice, ssk, *k6 (9, 11), k2tog, yo twice, ssk; rep from * once, k3, sm, k to end of row at lower-left front edge, slipping the rem markers as you go.
Row 7 (WS): Knit to the end of the row, slipping markers and knitting into the back of the loops of the yarn overs from the previous row.
Rows 8–11: Knit.
Do not cut yarn.

Collar
NOTE: The collar is worked with short rows. For a complete discussion of this technique, see page 154.

Row 1 (RS): Beg at the base of the right front, k84 (97, 110) sts to the third marker (the left shoulder), sm, k1, w&t the next stitch.

Row 2: Knit back to the marker at the left shoulder, sm, k28 (33, 38) (back of neck stitches), sm at right shoulder, k1, w&t next stitch.
Row 3: Knit back to the marker at the right shoulder, sm, k28 (33, 38), sm, k3, w&t next stitch.
Row 4: Knit back to the marker at the left shoulder, sm, k28 (33, 38), sm, k3, w&t next stitch.
Rows 5–16 (18, 22): Continue in the patt established in Rows 1–4, always knitting 1 st beyond the wrapped stitch from the previous row and then w&t the next stitch.
Row 17 (19, 23) (RS): Knit all the way down to the left front bodice edge.
Cut yarn. Do not BO; instead leave the stitches on the needle.

Vine Trim
The trim for this sweater is formed by knitting I-cord and simultaneously attaching it to the live stitches of the buttonhole band, the collar, and the button band.

First, several inches of I-cord are knitted without attaching it to the sweater. This will form the vine spiral on the right front of the sweater. The vine begins as a 2-stitch I-cord and is increased to 5-stitch I-cord.

With two US 5 dpns and color B, CO 2 sts.
Knit 2" (5cm) of I-cord.
Increase Row 1: K1, M1, k1—3 sts.
Knit 2" (5cm) of I-cord.
Increase Row 2: K1, M1, k2—4 sts.
Knit 2" (5cm) of I-cord.
Increase Row 3: K1, M1, k3—5 sts.
Knit 1" (5cm) of I-cord.

Attach the I-Cord
With the RS of the sweater facing you, begin attaching the I-cord at the lower edge of the right front bodice, continuing across the collar stitches, and working across the stitches of the left front, finally ending at the lower edge of the left front bodice.

Knit the first 4 sts of the next I-cord round, pick up the sweater (with RS facing) and hold the dpn with the rem I-cord stitch parallel and in front of the needle holding the sweater stitches. Insert the working dpn (the one holding the 4 I-cord sts) into both the rem I-cord stitch and the first stitch at the lower edge of the right front bodice. Knit these 2 sts together as if they were 1 st. You now have 5 sts on one dpn. Slide the 5 sts to the opposite end of the needle. The second dpn is empty. Using this dpn, work 4 sts of I-cord and then knit the fifth I-cord stitch and the next sweater stitch together. Continue in this manner, knitting 4 sts of I-cord and knitting the fifth I-cord stitch with the next sweater stitch until you are to the right collar (the first marker).

I-Cord Loops (Optional)

At the collar (between the first and fourth markers) continue to knit and attach I-cord, adding decorative loops as desired. Loops are made by working sections of attached I-cord alternated with sections of unattached I-cord. In other words, you will stop attaching the I-cord to the sweater edge for an inch or two, working plain I-cord for 1 or 2 inches, and then resume attaching the I-cord to the sweater.

To add these decorative loops, work attached I-cord to the place where you would like to make a loop. Knit a section of I-cord plain, without attaching it to the collar for ½" (1cm) to 2" (5cm). Once the unattached section is the desired length, rotate the I-cord needle clockwise 360 degrees twice before the beg of the next round. Resume attaching I-cord to collar. Continue working attached and unattached I-cord, stopping and placing loops at random. The number of loops on the collar and the number of attached I-cord stitches worked between them is completely discretionary.

After working to the fourth marker (the beg of the button band), stop adding decorative loops and attach each row of I-cord to the sweater stitches of the left front down to the base of the left front bodice.

Once you have reached the base of the left front bodice, BO the rem I-cord stitches. Cut yarn and fasten off.

Leaves

With two US 4 dpns and color B, CO 1 st.
Row 1: K1, p1, k1 in the same st—3 sts.
Row 2 and all even rows: Knit.
Row 3: K1, yo, k1, yo, k1—5 sts.
Row 5: K2, yo, k1, yo, k2—7 sts.
Row 7: K3, yo, k1, yo, k3—9 sts.
Row 9: K4, yo, k1, yo, k4—11 sts.
Row 11: Ssk, k7, k2tog—9 sts.
Row 13: Ssk, k5, k2tog—7 sts.
Row 15: Ssk, k3, k2tog—5 sts.
Row 17: Ssk, k1, k2tog—3 sts.
Row 19: Sk2po—1 st.

Cut yarn and pull through the rem stitch. Make six more leaves.

Flowers

With 16" US 5 needle and color A, CO 10 sts.
Row 1: Knit.
Row 2 and all even rows: Purl.
Row 3: Kfb across—20 sts.
Row 5: Rep Row 3—40 sts.
Row 7: Rep Row 3—80 sts.
Row 8: Purl.
BO stitches, leaving a 10" (25cm) tail for sewing the flower together.

Weave in ends.
Roll flower up like a cinnamon roll.
Thread a tapestry needle with the tail of the bound-off edge and sew the bottom edge of the flower together so that it maintains its shape.
Make four more flowers, two each in colors C and D.

Finishing

Weave in all ends.
Pin the I-cord tail to the sweater coat at the base of the buttonhole band and up onto the right bodice front, arranging it so that it spirals and twists like a vine. Sew into place.
Block sweater.
Sew leaves and flowers onto collar as shown in photos. Sew buttons opposite buttonholes.

Cloche

This hat is made in sturdy, stretchy garter stitch. Waste yarn is used to work the chained cast-on, and the hat is worked in the round from the bottom edge up. After the body of the hat is complete, the waste yarn from the cast-on edge is removed and an I-cord hatband is worked onto the live stitches at the lower edge of the hat. Knitted flowers and leaves embellish the body of the hat.

SIZES
0–6 months (6–18 months, 2–4 years, 4–6 years)

FINISHED MEASUREMENTS
Circumference: 12 (13, 16, 17^1/$_2$)" [30 (33, 41, 44)cm]

Sample size 2–4 years

MATERIALS
Knit Picks *Swish DK* (100% superwash wool; 123 yd. [112m] per 50g skein): #24051 Petal (color A), 1 (2, 2, 2) skeins; #24058 Asparagus (color B), 1 skein; #24052 Cornflower (color C), 1 skein; #24049 Eggplant (color D), 1 skein

US 5 (3.75mm) 12" circular needle for smaller sizes

US 5 (3.75mm) 16" circular needle for largest size

US 5 (3.75mm) double-pointed needles

US 4 (3.5mm) double-pointed needles

US size F (3.75mm) crochet hook

2 yd. (2m) smooth DK weight cotton yarn

Stitch markers

Tapestry needle

Row counter

GAUGE
22 sts and 42 rows = 4" (10cm) in garter stitch on US 5 (3.75mm) needles, or size needed to obtain gauge

STITCH PATTERNS
Garter stitch worked in the round—Knit a round, purl a round.

Chained cast-on (page 146)

I-cord (page 155)

K2tog (page 149)

Sk2po (page 151)

Ssk (page 150)

Kfb (page 148)

Yo (page 148)

SPECIAL TECHNIQUES
Attached I-cord (see instructions in this pattern)

Knitted flowers (see instructions in sweater coat pattern)

Knitted leaves (see instructions in sweater coat pattern)

Instructions
Hat Body

To work the cast-on used for this hat, you will need a length of waste yarn. It is important to choose a yarn that is smooth and will be easy to remove once the knitting is complete. Cotton yarn works best for this purpose since it is less likely to felt to the wool of the hat. Choose a scrap of yarn that is approximately 2 yd. (2m) long and is the same weight as the yarn used to knit the hat.

With crochet hook and US 5 needle, CO 64 (72, 88, 96) sts using chained cast-on (see page 146).

With color A, knit across CO stitches, pm, and join work in the round.

Work garter stitch in the round until work measures 4 (5, 6^1/$_2$, 7^1/$_2$)" [10 (13, 17, 19)cm], ending with a purl round.

Shape Top

Continue to use US 5 needle for top shaping, switching to dpns as needed.

Rnd 1: *K6, k2tog; rep from * 7 (8, 10, 11) times—56 (63, 77, 84) sts.

Rnd 2 and all even rounds: Purl.

Rnd 3: *K5, k2tog; rep from *—48 (54, 66, 72) sts.
Rnd 5: *K4, k2tog; rep from *—40 (45, 55, 60) sts.
Rnd 7: *K3, k2tog; rep from *—32 (36, 44, 48) sts.
Rnd 9: *K2, k2tog; rep from *—24 (27, 33, 36) sts.
Rnd 11: *K1, k2tog; rep from *—16 (18, 22, 24) sts.
Rnd 13: *K2tog; rep from *—8 (9, 11, 12) sts.
Rnd 15: For sizes 0–6 months and 4–6 years: *K2tog; rep from * to end—4 (6) sts. For sizes 6–18 months and 2–4 years: *K2tog; rep from * to last stitch, k1— 5 (6) sts.

Cut yarn, thread tail through rem stitches, and pull taut. Fasten off and weave in the tail on the WS of the hat.

I-Cord Hat Band

Carefully pull waste yarn out of CO edge, slipping stitches onto US 5 circular needle as you go. Put the hat aside and begin I-cord for the hat band.

With color B and US 4 dpns, CO 5 sts and work 3 rows of I-cord.

Attach the I-Cord

Knit the first 4 sts of the next I-cord round. Pick up the hat. With RS facing and starting at the beg of the round, hold the dpn with the rem I-cord stitch parallel and in front of the needle holding the hat stitches. Insert the working dpn (the one holding the 4 I-cord sts) into both the rem I-cord stitch and the first hat stitch. Knit these 2 sts together as if they were 1 st. You now have 5 sts on one dpn. Slide the 5 sts to the opposite end of the needle. The second dpn is empty. Using the empty dpn, work 4 sts of I-cord and knit the fifth I-cord stitch and the next hat stitch together.

I-Cord Loops

To create the ivy-like loops around the hat edge, you will alternate sections of attached I-cord with sections of I-cord knitted plain. Knit 1–2" (3–5cm) of attached I-cord up to the place where you want to position a loop and then work ½–2" (1–5cm) of I-cord without attaching it to the hat. Once you have made the I-cord the length desired for the loop, rotate the needle holding the I-cord stitches 360 degrees twice. Resume attaching the I-cord to the hat. Continue in this way, alternating sections of plain I-cord and attached I-cord, around the hat edge. The length of the attached and plain I-cord sections is completely discretionary. Make the loops as long and as often as you want to create a hat that is entirely your own.

I-Cord Vine

When you have reached the end of the round and the last hat stitch has been worked, do not cut yarn. Instead, continue working with the 5 I-cord sts. Knit 6½" (17cm) of unattached I-cord. Do not cut yarn.

Next rnd: K1, k2tog, k2—4 sts.
Work 3" (8cm) of 4-stitch I-cord.
Next rnd: K1, k2tog, k1—3 sts.
Work 3" (8cm) of 3-stitch I-cord.
Next rnd: K2tog, k1—2 sts.
Work 2½" (6cm) of 2-stitch I-cord.
Cut yarn, thread tail through rem stitches, and fasten off.

Sew the cast-on edge of the I-cord to the hat. Sew the long I-cord tail to the hat so that it curves and spirals like a vine. If you made any extra long I-cord loops, arrange them on the hat and sew in place if needed.

Flowers

With US 5 needle, make three flowers: one each in colors A, C, and D (see instructions in sweater coat pattern).

Leaves

With color B and US 5 dpns, make three leaves (see instructions in sweater coat pattern).

Finishing

Weave in all ends and block hat.
Sew the flowers and leaves to hat as desired using photos as a guide. Weave in rem loose ends.

Sundress

This outfit is made with both circular and flat knitting techniques and is worked from the peplum up. The peplum is constructed of four large leaves worked separately in garter stitch rows. After all four of the leaves have been completed, they are joined together in the round. The torso of the bodice is worked in a slip stitch pattern in the round to the armhole edge where stitches are divided for the front and back of the dress. From the armholes, the

work progresses in rows to the shoulder seams. A knitted flower and picot edging complete the neckline and armholes.

SIZES
6 months (12–18 months, 2 years, 3 years, 4 years)

FINISHED MEASUREMENTS
Chest: 18 (19, 20^1/$_2$, 22^1/$_2$, 24)" [46 (48, 52, 57, 61)cm]
Bodice length from shoulder: 11 (12, 12^1/$_2$, 13, 14)" [28 (30, 32, 33, 36)cm]

Sample size 3 years

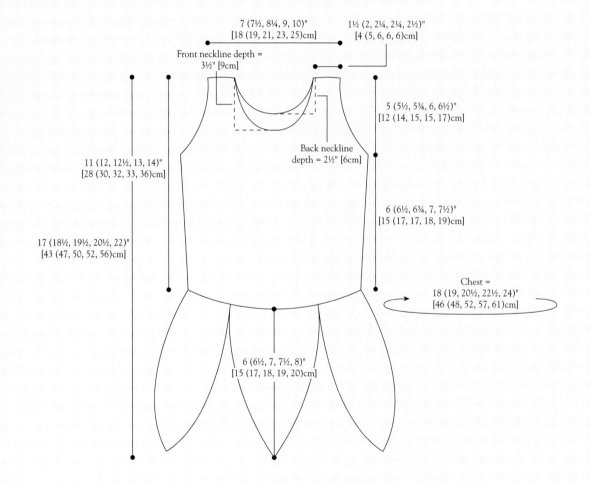

7 (7½, 8¼, 9, 10)"
[18 (19, 21, 23, 25)cm]

1½ (2, 2¼, 2¼, 2½)"
[4 (5, 6, 6, 6)cm]

Front neckline depth =
3½" [9cm]

5 (5½, 5¾, 6, 6½)"
[12 (14, 15, 15, 17)cm]

Back neckline
depth = 2½" [6cm]

11 (12, 12½, 13, 14)"
[28 (30, 32, 33, 36)cm]

6 (6½, 6¾, 7, 7½)"
[15 (17, 17, 18, 19)cm]

17 (18½, 19½, 20½, 22)"
[43 (47, 50, 52, 56)cm]

Chest =
18 (19, 20½, 22½, 24)"
[46 (48, 52, 57, 61)cm]

6 (6½, 7, 7½, 8)"
[15 (17, 18, 19, 20)cm]

MATERIALS

Knit Picks *CotLin* (70% tanguis cotton, 30% linen; 123 yd. [112m] per 50g skein): #696 Key Lime (color A), 2 (2, 2, 3, 3) skeins; #693 Fiesta Pink (color B), 2 (2, 2, 3, 3) skeins; #697 Royal Plum (color C), 1 skein

US 4 (3.5mm) 16" circular needle

US 4 (3.5mm) 24" circular needle

US 4 (3.5mm) double-pointed needles

US 3 (3.25mm) 16" circular needle (optional)

US 3 (3.25mm) double-pointed needles

Stitch markers

Stitch holders

Tapestry needle

Row counter

Sewing needle

Sewing thread to match yarn

GAUGE

22 sts and 40 rows = 4" (10cm) in garter stitch on US 4 (3.5mm) needles, or size needed to obtain gauge

25 sts and 34 rows = 4" (10cm) in slip stitch pattern on US 4 (3.5mm) needles, or size needed to obtain gauge

STITCH PATTERNS

Garter stitch worked flat—Knit all stitches every row.

Slip stitch pattern worked in the round—Work all odd rows: *k3 (4, 3, 4, 3), sl 1; rep from * to end. Knit all even rows.

Slip stitch pattern worked flat—Work all odd rows: *k3 (4, 3, 4, 3), sl 1; rep from * to end. Purl all even rows.

Cable cast-on (page 146)

K2tog (page 149)

Ssk (page 150)

SPECIAL TECHNIQUES

Three-needle bind-off (page 151)

Bobble (see instructions in this pattern)

Knitted flower (see instructions in this pattern)

Knitted picot bind-off edging (see instructions in this pattern)

Instructions

Peplum

With color A and US 4 16" needle, CO 1 st.

Row 1 (RS): K1, p1, k1 in same stitch—3 sts.

Row 2: Knit.

Row 3: Yo, k to end—4 sts.

Rows 4–55 (4–59, 4–63, 4–69, 4–75): Rep Row 3 until 56 (60, 64, 70, 76) sts are on the needle.

Cut yarn. Put the leaf on a holder and rep the rows above three more times for a total of four leaves.

Join leaves (WS): Place leaves on 24" US 4 needle, arranging them so that the tail of each leaf is trailing from the RH side of the work. With WS facing, knit across all four leaves joining them together as you go—224 (240, 256, 280, 304) sts.

Join peplum in the round: Turn work so that the RS is facing and pm. Join work in the round and purl.

Gather peplum: Using 16" US 4 needle for sizes 6 months–3 years and 24" US 4 needle for the largest size, *k2tog; rep from * to end—112 (120, 128, 140, 152) sts. Cut yarn A.

Bodice

As you begin the bodice, you will need to arrange the leaves so that they are centered at the front, back, and sides of the dress. This will change the beg and end of the round. The marker that you place in the following round marks the beg of the bodice round at the left side of the dress.

Slip 14 (15, 16, 17, 19) sts from the LH to the RH needle. Place a new marker. This is the beg of the round and the left side "seam."

Join color B.

K56 (60, 64, 70, 76) sts and place a contrasting marker to indicate the right side "seam." Continue knitting to the end of the round, discarding the marker that was placed when you joined the peplum in the round and slipping the two new markers as you go. The bodice is worked in the round from here up to the armholes.

Slip Stitch Pattern

Rnd 1: *K3 (4, 3, 4, 3), sl 1; rep from * to end.

Rnd 2: Knit.

Rep last two rounds until piece measures 6 (6½, 6¾, 7, 7½)" [15 (17, 17, 18, 19)cm] from beg of the bodice, ending with Rnd 2.

Divide for Front and Back

From this point on, the bodice is worked back and forth in rows. You will work the front of the bodice first. The stitches for the back of the bodice will be held in reserve for later.

Front Armhole Shaping

Row 1 (RS): BO 4 sts for the left underarm. Work in established sl st pattern to marker (right underarm)—52 (56, 60, 66, 72) sts.
Place rem 56 (60, 64, 70, 76) sts on a holder for the bodice back.
Row 2 (WS): BO 4 sts pwise for right underarm, p to the end of the row—48 (52, 56, 62, 68) sts.
Row 3 (RS): K1, ssk, work in patt to last 3 sts, k2tog, k1—46 (50, 54, 60, 66) sts.
Row 4: Purl.
Rep last two rows 1 (1, 1, 2, 2) time(s)—44 (48, 52, 56, 62) sts.

Continue to work in patt without further shaping until armhole measures 1½ (2, 2¼, 2½, 3)" [4 (5, 6, 6, 8)cm], ending with a WS row.

Divide for Neck

Next row (RS): Work in patt across first 15 (17, 19, 20, 22) sts for left front and shoulder, BO 14 (14, 14, 16, 18) sts for center front of neck, work rem 15 (17, 19, 20, 22) sts for right front and shoulder in patt.

Put the stitches for the left shoulder on a holder to be worked later.

Right Front Neckline

Row 1 (WS): Beg at the right armhole, p15 (17, 19, 20, 22) sts to the right neck edge.
Row 2 (RS): Ssk (at neck edge), work in patt to end of row (right armhole edge)—14 (16, 18, 19, 21) sts.
Rep last two rows 4 (4, 4, 5, 5) times—10 (12, 14, 14, 16) sts.

Continue to work in patt without decreasing until the armhole measures 5 (5½, 5¾, 6, 6½)" [13 (14, 15, 15, 17)cm], ending with a RS row.
Put rem 10 (12, 14, 14, 16) sts on a holder.

Left Front Neckline

Slide stitches on reserve for left shoulder onto 16" US 4 needle.
Join a second ball of yarn at left neck edge.
Row 1 (WS): P15 (17, 19, 20, 22) sts to the left armhole.
Row 2 (RS): Work in patt to last 2 sts, k2tog (at neck edge)—14 (16, 18, 19, 21) sts.
Rep last two rows 4 (4, 4, 5, 5) times—10 (12, 14, 14, 16) sts.

Continue to work in patt without decreasing until the armhole measures 5 (5½, 5¾, 6, 6½)" [13 (14, 15, 15, 17)cm], ending with a RS row.
Put rem 10 (12, 14, 14, 16) sts on a holder.

Bodice Back

Slide the 56 (60, 64, 70, 76) sts on reserve for the bodice back onto US 4 needle (you can use either the 16 " or 24"). Join new skein of yarn at the right underarm.

Back Armhole Shaping

Beg with a RS row, shape armholes as for front—44 (48, 52, 56, 62) sts.

Work in established patt until armhole measures 2½ (3, 3¼, 3½, 4)" [6 (8, 8, 9, 10)cm], ending with a WS row.

Back Neckline

With RS facing, work 15 (17, 19, 20, 22) sts for the right front and shoulder in patt, BO 14 (14, 14, 16, 18) sts for the center neckline, work rem 15 (17, 19, 20, 22) sts for the left shoulder.

Put 15 (17, 19, 20, 22) sts for the right shoulder on a holder for later.

Left Back Neckline

Row 1 (WS): P15 (17, 19, 20, 22) sts from the left armhole edge to neck opening.
Row 2 (RS): Ssk (at neck edge), work in patt to end of row (left armhole edge)—14 (16, 18, 19, 21) sts.
Rep last two rows 4 (4, 4, 5, 5) times—10 (12, 14, 14, 16) sts.

Continue to work in patt without decreasing until the armhole measures 5 (5½, 5¾, 6, 6½)" [13 (14, 15, 15, 17)cm], ending with a WS row.

Put rem 10 (12, 14, 14, 16) sts on a holder.

Right Back Neckline
Slide stitches on reserve for right shoulder onto 16" US 4 needle.
Join a second ball of yarn at the right neckline edge.
Row 1 (WS): P15 (17, 19, 20, 22) sts to the right armhole.
Row 2 (RS): Work in patt to last 2 sts, k2tog (at neck edge)—14 (16, 18, 19, 21) sts.
Rep last two rows 4 (4, 4, 5, 5) times—10 (12, 14, 14, 16) sts.

Continue to work in patt until the back and the front are equal in length, ending with a WS row.

Shoulder Seams

Turn the sweater inside out so that the RS of the sweater are together. Place each set of shoulder stitches onto a separate US 4 dpn. With WS of dress front facing and beg at the right armhole edge, join color B and work a three-needle bind-off to join the right shoulder stitches together. Cut yarn and fasten off.

Rep for left shoulder seam, working from the armhole to the neck edge.

Neckband

To work the neckband, you will pick up and knit stitches around the neckline opening. With RS facing and beg at left shoulder seam, use US 3 dpns and color B to pick up and knit approximately 3 sts for every 4 sts of the neckline edge, ending with an even number of stitches. Try to pick up approximately the same number of stitches on the left and right sides of the neckline, making sure that the stitches are evenly spaced around the neckline opening.

Arrange the stitches evenly on the dpns, pm, join the work in a round, and purl 1 round.

Picot Bind-Off
BO 2 sts kwise, *slide the stitch rem on the right needle back to the left needle. CO 3 sts using cable cast-on (see page 146). BO 5 sts; rep from * to the end of the round. Cut yarn and fasten off end.

Armbands

With RS of work facing and beg at left underarm, use US 3 dpns and color B to pick up and knit approximately 3 sts for every 4 sts around the armhole edge, ending with an even number of stitches. As you do this make sure that you pick up the same number of stitches for the front and back of the dress, and that the stitches are evenly spaced around the armhole opening. Arrange the stitches evenly on the dpns, pm, join the work in a round, and purl 1 round.

Work Picot Bind-off around armhole edge as you did for the neck opening.

Rep for right armband.

Flower

With color C and US 4 dpns, CO 6 sts.
Rows 1–3: Knit.
Row 4: Sl 1, k3, using the tip of the left needle, lift the second, third, and fourth stitch over the first stitch, k2 sts rem on left needle—3 sts.
Row 5: Knit.
Row 6: CO 3 sts, k to end—6 sts.
Rep Rows 1–6 four more times for a total of 30 rows. Work one last repeat of patt through Row 5.

BO the final 3 sts. Cut yarn, leaving a 10" (25cm) tail and fasten off rem stitch.

Thread the tail through a tapestry needle, and run it through the base of the flower petals (the straight edge). Pull tightly, drawing the flower together. Use the rem yarn to connect the first and the last petal together in a round. Fasten off yarn and weave in ends.

Leaves

With two strands of color A held together and with US 4 dpns, CO 8 sts, turn.

BO 8 sts, leaving last stitch on needle. Do not cut yarn. Use the working yarn and the backward loop method (page 145) to CO 7 more sts, turn, BO 8 sts. Cut yarn, fasten off rem st, and weave in ends.

Rep for second leaf.

Bobble

With color B and US 4 dpns, CO 1 st.
Row 1: Knit into the front, back, front, back, and front again of stitch—5 sts. Turn.
Rows 2 and 4: Knit.
Rows 3 and 5: Purl.

Do not turn work after the last row.
Use the empty dpn to lift the second, third, fourth, and fifth stitch (one at a time) over the first stitch—1 st.
Cut yarn, leaving a 12" (30cm) tail. Fasten off.
Tie the tails from the CO and BO edges together to gather the bobble. Thread a tapestry needle with one of the tails and weave it into the bobble. You will use the second tail to sew the bobble to the flower.

Finishing

Weave in all ends. Block dress.
Layer the bobble on top of the flower and sew in place.
Place the leaves under the flower and sew the flower and leaves to bodice front.

Elves

The design for these fanciful slippers and holiday stocking was inspired by the Grimm Brothers' tale "The Elves and the Shoemaker," and just like the cobbler in the story, you will find that everyone wants a pair of these warm and sturdy boots. Fortunately, you can knit this pattern in no time! Knit in wool and felted to a dense fabric, these cozy slippers are designed to keep little feet toasty and warm from ankle to toes. The extra long leg of the stocking is just right for holding generous supplies of holiday sweets and goodies. Full of fun and whimsical details, these elf boots make a wonderful gift for fairy folk of all kinds. Knit them in a rainbow of colors for all the wee ones in your life.

Slippers and Holiday Stocking

This design is a variation of a traditional sock pattern and is worked in the round from the top down. The triangle trim at the top of the slipper and stocking is worked first. Each triangle is worked flat, in garter stitch. After all of the triangles are complete, a purl row unites the triangles to one another and the work is joined in the round. The upper leg of the piece is bordered by two welts or folds of reverse stockinette stitch. These folds can be worked as part of the pattern or can be sewn in place after the project is complete. The rest of the slipper/stocking is worked like a regular sock to the toe. The curl at the end of the toe is formed by a series of short rows.

SIZES
Slipper: 12–18 months (2 years, 4 years)
Stocking: One size

FINISHED MEASUREMENTS (AFTER FELTING)
Foot length from back of heel to turn of the toe
12–18 months: 5" (13cm)
2 years: 6" (15cm)
4 years: 7$\frac{1}{2}$" (19cm)
Stocking: 9" (23cm)

Height from slipper sole to upper edge
12–18 months: 4$\frac{1}{2}$" (11cm)
2 years: 4$\frac{1}{2}$" (11cm)
4 years: 5" (13cm)
Stocking: 15" (38cm)

MATERIALS
Cascade Yarns *220* (100% Peruvian Highland wool; 220 yd. [201m] per 100g hank): #8903 Lime Green, #9488 Heather Red, #8891 Turquoise, #8886 Eggplant, #7808 Purple, #7818 Royal Blue. Each pair of slippers and stocking requires three accent colors (partial hanks of each) and 1 (1, 2, 2) hanks main color.
US 10 (6mm) double-pointed needles
Row counter
Stitch holder
Stitch markers
Tapestry needle
Ribbon for hanging stocking (optional)

COLORS
Each slipper is made of one main color (MC) and three contrasting colors (CC1, CC2, and CC3). Listed below are the sample color combinations and their respective sizes.
12–18 months: MC—Heather Red, CC1—Turquoise, CC2—Lime, CC3—Purple
2 years: MC—Turquoise, CC1—Heather Red, CC2—Lime, CC3—Eggplant
4 years: MC—Royal blue, CC1—Lime, CC2—Eggplant, CC3—Turquoise
Stocking: MC—Lime, CC1—Heather Red, CC2—Eggplant, CC3—Turquoise

GAUGE BEFORE FELTING
16 sts and 20 rows = 4" (10cm) in St st on US 10 (6mm) needles, or size needed to obtain gauge

NOTE: Cascade Yarns 220 is typically worked on US 7 or 8 needles at a much tighter gauge (4$\frac{1}{2}$ or 5 sts to the inch). The gauge for this project is looser and is worked on larger needles to facilitate the felting process.

STITCH PATTERNS
Garter stitch worked flat—Knit all stitches every row.
Stockinette stitch worked in the round—Knit all stitches every round.
Reverse stockinette stitch worked in the round—Purl all stitches every round.
W&t (page 154)
K2tog (page 149)
P2tog (page 150)
Ssk (page 150)
Kfb (page 148)

SPECIAL TECHNIQUES
Bobbles (see instructions in this pattern)
Short rows (page 154)
Felting (page 160)

Instructions
NOTE: The sizes in the pattern are listed as follows: 12–18 months (2 years, 4 years, stocking).

Triangles
The 4 (5, 6, 7) triangles decorating the upper border are knit first. They are worked back and forth in rows on dpns. CO 2 sts using CC1.
Row 1: Knit.
Row 2: Kfb, k to end—3 sts.

Rep last row 6 (5, 5, 5) times—9 (8, 8, 8) sts. Cut yarn, leaving a long tail for weaving in later.

Make 3 (4, 5, 6) more triangles as above. You should be able to fit two to three triangles on a dpn. Use additional needles as necessary.

NOTE: Here is a trick to keep all of your triangles facing the same direction. For 8-stitch triangles, turn the work before casting on the next triangle and cast on at the opposite end of the needle (the tail from the last triangle made will be trailing off of the left edge of the work). For 9-stitch triangles, do not turn work, instead push the triangle just completed down the needle and cast on the next triangle beside it (the tail from the previous triangle will be trailing from the RH side of the triangle).

After 4 (5, 6, 7) triangles are complete, arrange work so that all of the triangles are facing the same way.

Join Triangles

With the work facing so that the tail of each triangle is trailing from the right edge of the triangle, join CC2 and purl across all of the triangles, connecting them to one another—36 (40, 48, 56) sts. This is the base of the triangle edging. It will be referenced later in the Border section of the pattern.

Divide stitches evenly on three dpns.

Border

The border of the slipper/stocking is worked in three sections: the upper edging, the center, and the lower edging.

Upper Edging

NOTE: You will work in the round from here to the heel flap.

Place a marker and join work in the round.
Rnds 1–8: Continuing with CC2, knit. Cut yarn.
Rnd 9: In this round you will create a welt or tube of reverse stockinette stitch by folding the work upward and joining stitches from the base of the triangle edging to Rnd 8.

With the tip of the LH needle, pick up the first stitch of the base of the triangle edging. To find this stitch, follow the first stitch on the LH needle down the front of the work eight rounds. This is the base of the triangle edging and the row you purled when joining the triangles together. Insert the tip of the LH needle into the first purl stitch of this row (from the base of the stitch up and from left to right), picking the stitch up and placing it on the left needle.

Join CC3. Insert the tip of the RH needle, from left to right, into the front of both the first live stitch on the LH needle and the stitch just placed there. Knit these 2 sts together. Continue the round in this manner, picking up a stitch from the base of the triangle edging below and knitting it together with the corresponding stitch from Rnd 8.

When you have completed this round, the purl side of Rnds 1–8 will be facing you, the tube of knitting you just created will be hanging down from the needle, and the live stitches on the needle will be behind the triangles. The points of the triangles will be pointing up.

NOTE: The next few rounds might feel a little awkward since you will be knitting behind the triangles. After the first round, the knitting becomes much easier.

Center Section

Still using CC3, work St st for 10 rounds. Cut yarn.

Lower Edging

Rnd 1: Join CC2 and knit. This is the base round for the second welt.

Rnds 2–7: Work in reverse stockinette stitch, purling all stitches. Cut yarn.
Join MC.
Rnd 8: In this round you will be creating a tube of knitting similar to the one made in the upper edge. With the tip of the LH needle, reach around to the back of the work and pick up the first stitch of Rnd 1, the base round of the second welt. The stitch will appear as a purl from the WS of the work. Knit this stitch together with the first live stitch on the LH needle. Continue as established to end of round.

NOTE: If you would rather sew the welts in place after the knitting is complete, ignore the instructions for Rnd 9 of the Upper Edging and Rnd 8 of the Lower Edging and knit these rounds in St st instead. After the boot is complete fold the triangle trim down to Rnd 9 of the Upper Edging and whipstitch (see page 153) in place with a length of matching yarn. Turn the boot inside out and close the second welt by stitching Rnds 1 and 8 of the Lower Edging together.

Leg

For the slipper, work two rounds in St st.
For the stocking, work St st until work measures 18" (46cm) from upper edge.

Heel Flap

The heel flap is worked back and forth in rows.
Row 1: K9 (10, 12, 14), turn.
Row 2: P18 (20, 24, 28), turn, and work on these stitches only for heel flap, putting the rem 18 (20, 24, 28) instep sts onto a holder for later.
Row 3 (RS): Sl 1, k17 (19, 23, 27).
Row 4: Sl 1, p17 (19, 23, 27).
Rep last two rows 7 (8, 10, 13) times.

Because the first stitch at the beg of every row was a slip stitch, there should be 8 (9, 11, 14) long sts on each selvedge of the heel flap.

Turn the Heel

You will use a series of short rows to turn and shape the heel.
Row 1 (RS): K11 (12, 14, 16), ssk, k1, turn.

Row 2: Sl 1, p5, p2tog, p1, turn.
Row 3: Sl 1, k6 to the last stitch before the gap that was formed when you turned the work in the previous row, ssk (with 1 st from each side of gap), k1, turn.
Row 4: Sl 1, p7 (to last stitch before gap), p2tog (with 1 st from each side of gap), p1, turn.

Continue in patt established in Rows 3 and 4 slipping the first stitch of every row, working one more stitch in the middle of each row, and dec with the stitches on either side of the gap formed on the previous row. Continue in this manner until all of the heel stitches have been worked, ending with a WS row—12 (12, 14, 16) sts rem. Do not cut yarn.

Heel Gusset

Knit across 12 (12, 14, 16) rem heel stitches.
With a separate needle, pick up and k9 (10, 12, 14) sts along the left selvedge of the heel flap.

Using a second needle, k across the 18 (20, 24, 28) instep sts from holder.

Using a third needle, pick up and k across 9 (10, 12, 14) sts along the right selvedge of the heel flap.

The remainder of the heel gusset is worked in the round. Rearrange the 48 (52, 62, 72) sts on three dpns as follows:

Needle 1: The 6 (6, 7, 8) sts from the left half of the heel along with the 9 (10, 12, 14) sts picked up from the left selvedge of the heel flap.
Needle 2: The 18 (20, 24, 28) instep sts (the top of the foot).
Needle 3: The 9 (10, 12, 14) sts picked up from the right selvedge of the heel flap, together with the rem 6 (6, 7, 8) heel stitches.
The beg of the round is at the center of the heel stitches (between needles 1 and 3).
Rnd 1: Knit.
Rnd 2: K to the last 3 sts on needle 1, k2tog, k1; k across instep sts (needle 2); k1, ssk, k to end of needle 3—46 (50, 60, 70) sts.
Rem gusset rnds: Rep Rnds 1 and 2 until the original number of stitches is restored—36 (40, 48, 56) sts.

Foot

Work in St st until piece measures 6½ (7¾, 9½, 11)" [17 (20, 24, 28)cm] from back of heel.

Toe Shaping

Short rows create the curled toe of the boot. To work the toe, the slipper is divided into two halves, the top half made up of the instep stitches (all the stitches on needle 2) and the bottom half, consisting of the rem stitches (all the stitches on needles 1 and 3).

NOTE: For complete discussion of short-row techniques, see page 154.

Preparatory Row: K across the 9 (10, 12, 14) sts on needle 1; w&t the next stitch (on needle 2).
Row 1: P across the 18 (20, 24, 28) sts on needles 1 and 3 (the bottom half of the slipper); w&t the next stitch (from needle 2).

Row 2: Knit across the 18 (20, 24, 28) sts on needles 3 and 1. You are now at the left end of needle 1 and at beg of needle 2, and in position to work the Dec Rnd.

Dec Rnd: Beg at needle 2, k2tog (the first 2 sts on this needle); k to the last 2 sts on needle 2, ssk. Ssk the first 2 sts on needle 3. K to the last 2 sts of needle 1, k2tog, w&t next stitch (from needle 2).

Continue as established above, working Rows 1 and 2 followed by a Dec Rnd until 6 or fewer sts rem. Cut yarn, leaving a 10" (25cm) tail. Fasten off the toe by threading a tapestry needle with the tail and running it through the rem live stitches. Turn the piece inside out and weave in the end of the tail.

Bobbles

Make 10 (12, 14, 16) bobbles.
CO 1 st in color of choice.
Knit into the front, back, front, and back again of the same stitch—4 sts.

Turn work, p4, turn, k4, turn, p2tog twice, turn, k2tog—1 st. Cut yarn, leaving a 10" (25cm) tail to sew the bobble to the slipper/stocking. Pull the tail through rem stitch and fasten off.

Finishing

Weave in all loose ends. Sew one bobble to each triangle point and to the end of the toe.

Felting

Felt elf boots in the washing machine per the felting instructions on page 160. Stuff with plastic bags to block into desired shape. Air-dry.

Hanging Tab for Stocking

Cut a 4–6" (10–15cm) length of ribbon for the hanging tab and fold it in half. Pin the cut ends of the ribbon to the upper-inside edge of the stocking. Sew in place.

Magic Carpets

Destination dreamland … and what could be more thrilling than arriving on a magic carpet? Your little one will sail above the clouds into worlds of imagination and dreams of adventure with these colorful blankets. Made in warm wool, these blankets are a dream come true, just right for days of creative play and nights of peaceful slumber.

Starry Night Blanket

Your child will love snuggling under the constellation of bright stars on this cozy blanket. Inspired by traditional patchwork quilt patterns and embellished with flying carpet tassels, this celestial design appeals to little and big kids alike. It is made of soft, worsted weight yarn and is sized to keep your child wrapped in wooly goodness from infancy to grade school. Perfect for naptime, playtime or curling up with a good book, this versatile blankie is bound to be a favorite friend for years to come.

Striped Blanket

Sweet dreams and hours of creative play are just around the corner with this magic carpet blanket. Inspired by kilim rugs and Persian carpets, this nontraditional design is a really fun knitting project. The size and shape of this blanket are perfect for crib, cot, stroller, and car seat. This whimsical blanket will keep your child happy and warm wherever he goes.

Starry Night Blanket

The center panel of this blanket is made first. It is worked flat with intarsia colorwork. After the panel is complete, selvedge stitches are picked up and worked in garter stitch rounds to form the blanket border. This blanket could be worked with a plain, patterned, or striped panel and embellished with duplicate-stitch stars or other pattern motifs.

FINISHED MEASUREMENTS
22¹⁄₂" × 28¹⁄₂" (57cm × 72cm)

MATERIALS
Cascade Yarns *220* (100% Peruvian Highland wool; 220 yd. [201m] per 100g skein): #7818 Royal Blue (color A), 2 skeins; 1 skein each #7812 Deco Green (color B), #8891 Turquoise (color C), #7814 Lime (color D), #7824 Orange (color E), #9470 Fuchsia (color F), #9422 Red (color G), #9463B Yellow (color H), #7808 Purple (color I), #9478 Soft Pink (color J), #8910 Key Lime (color K).
US 6 (4mm) 32" circular needle
US 6 (4mm) 40" circular needle
8 stitch markers, including 1 of contrasting color
Row counter
Bobbins (optional)
Tapestry needle
4" × 4" (10cm × 10cm) piece of cardboard

GAUGE
18 sts and 24 rows = 4" (10cm) in St st on US 6 (4mm) needles, or size needed to obtain gauge

STITCH PATTERNS
Stockinette stitch worked flat—Knit on RS rows; purl on WS rows.
Garter stitch worked in the round—Knit a round, purl a round.
M1 (page 149)

SPECIAL TECHNIQUES
Intarsia (page 157)
Tassels (see instructions in this pattern)

Instructions

In preparation for working the center panel, wind one or two bobbins of each contrast color (colors B–K). Depending on the size of your bobbins, you may need to wind additional bobbins as you work the center panel.

Center Panel

With 32" needle and color A, CO 81 sts.
Work 6 rows in St st.

Work Chart

NOTE: Download a full-size version of the Starry Night Blanket chart at www.wiley.com/go/fairytaleknits.

The chart for the center panel (see the next page) is worked from the bottom up, from right to left on RS rows and left to right on WS rows. Work the chart in St st, beg with a RS row and using intarsia for the colorwork.

NOTE: Because you do not carry the yarn across the back of the work when changing colors in intarsia, you will need to twist the yarns together to prevent a hole forming where the color change occurs. To do this on RS rows, pick up the new yarn from underneath the yarn just used. On WS rows, drop the yarn just used and bring the new yarn up and to the right of the yarn just used to twist the yarns.

Finish Center Panel

Using color A only, work in St st for 6 rows, ending with a WS row.
Cut color A.

Border

The border of the blanket is worked in the round. To do this you will pick up stitches along the four sides and a single stitch at each corner of the center panel. You will then knit around, increasing at the corners every other round until the border is complete.

With RS facing, color B and 40" needle, k1, pm, k79, pm, k1, pm. Do not turn work. Rotate the piece clockwise and pick up 110 sts evenly along the side edge, pm, pick up 1 st

at corner, pm. Rotate the work, pick up 79 sts evenly along third side edge, pm, pick up 1 corner st, pm. Rotate the work for the third time and pick up 110 sts evenly along rem edge of panel. Place contrasting marker—382 sts.

Rnd 1: *K1, sm, M1, purl to marker, M1, sm; rep from * around to contrasting marker (8 sts increased)—390 sts.
Rnd 2: Knit.
Rnds 3, 5, 7, 9, 11, and 13: Rep Rnd 1.
Rnds 4, 6, 8, 10, and 12: Rep Rnd 2.
You should now have 438 sts. Cut color B. Join color A and work remainder of border in color A as follows.
Rnd 14: Rep Rnd 2.
Rnd 15: Rep Rnd 1—446 sts.
BO kwise.

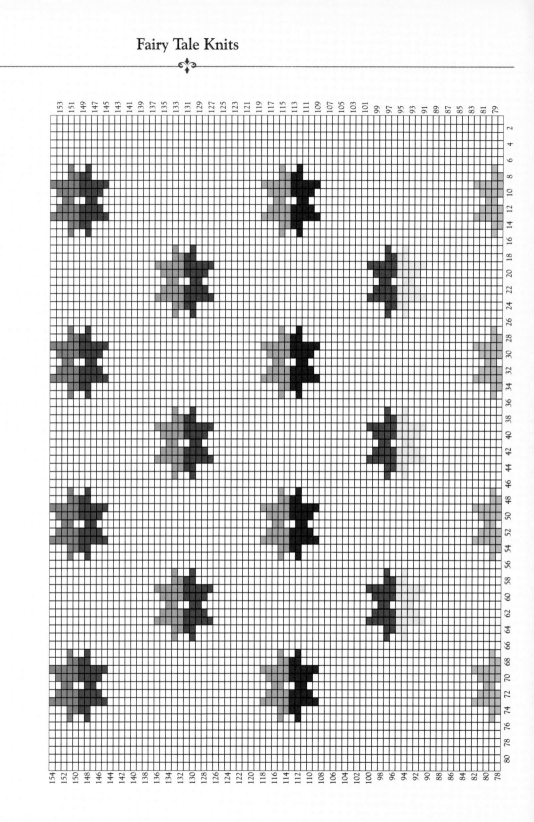

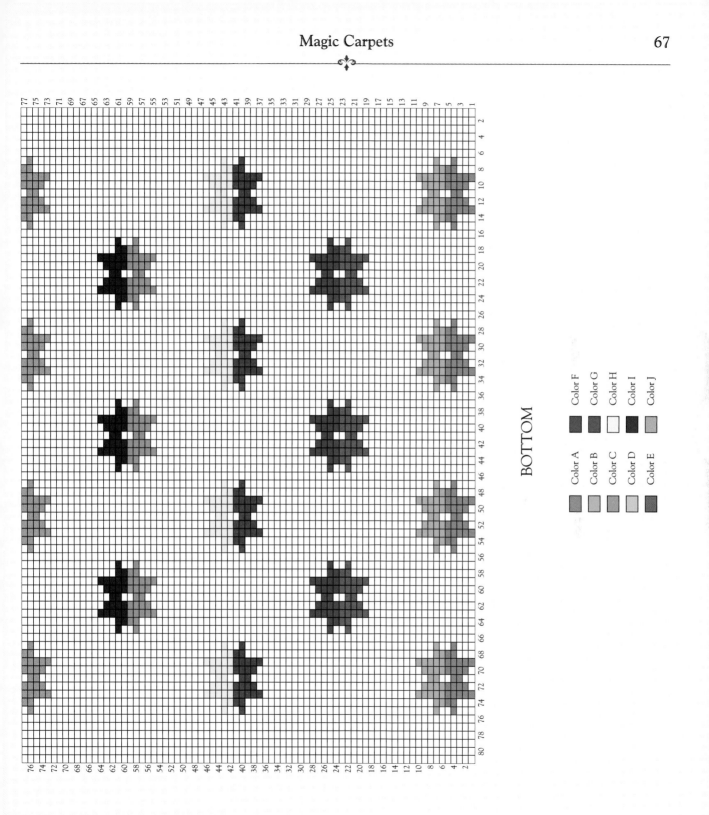

BOTTOM

Color A
Color B
Color C
Color D
Color E
Color F
Color G
Color H
Color I
Color J

Tassels

Use colors E and F to make four tassels. Wrap color F around the 4" piece of cardboard 50 times, layering it on top of itself. Cut yarn so that the tail end is even with the lower edge of the cardboard. Rep with the color E, stacking it on top of the color F bundle. Cut two 12" (30cm) lengths of yarn E. Take one length and thread it under the yarn bundle at the upper end of the cardboard. Tie a knot tightly around the end of the bundle. Do not cut the ends of this tie; they will be used to sew the tassel onto the blanket later.

Gently remove the yarn bundle from the cardboard. Wrap the second length of yarn around the entire bundle approximately 1" (3cm) down from the first tie. Knot the end and then turn the bundle over and tie a knot on the other side. Weave the ends of this tie into the bundle. Cut the loops at the lower end of the bundle and trim to desired length.

Finishing

Weave in all ends. Block blanket. Sew tassels to blanket corners.

Striped Blanket

This blanket is worked as a single panel and is knit on the bias. After the panel is complete, stitches are picked up around the four edges of the piece. Garter stitch and Fair Isle bands, worked in the round, frame the center panel and form the border of the blanket. Garter stitch triangles knitted out from the border stitches complete the blanket.

FINISHED MEASUREMENTS
28" × 28" (71cm × 71cm) without triangle trim

MATERIALS
Cascade Yarns *220* (100% Peruvian Highland wool; 220 yd. [201m] per 100g skein): #8891 Turquoise (color A), 2 skeins; #7814 Lime (color B), 2 skeins; #7818 Royal Blue (color C), #9470 Fuchsia (color D), #7824 Orange (color E), 1 skein of each colors C, D, and E
US 6 (4mm) 24" circular needle
US 6 (4mm) 40" circular needle
8 stitch markers, including 1 of contrasting color
Row counter
Tapestry needle
4" × 4" (10cm × 10cm) piece of cardboard

GAUGE
18 sts and 24 rows = 4" (10cm) in St st on US 6 (4mm) needles, or size needed to obtain gauge

STITCH PATTERNS
Garter stitch worked flat—Knit all stitches every row.
Garter stitch worked in the round—Knit one round; purl one round.
Stockinette stitch worked in the round—Knit all stitches every round.
K2tog (page 149)
Ssk (page 150)
Kfb (page 148)

SPECIAL TECHNIQUES
French knots (page 156)
Pompoms (page 155)
Fair Isle colorwork (page 157)

Instructions
Center Panel

The center panel is knit on the bias beg with a corner stitch and working on the diagonal from there.

With 24" needle and color A, CO 1 st.
Row 1 (RS): Kfb—2 sts.
Rows 2–10: Kfb, k to end—11 sts.

Change to color B.
Rows 11–20: Kfb, k to end—21 sts.

Change back to color A.
Rows 21–110: Continue as established, inc 1 st at the beg of every row, and alternating 10 rows of color A with 10 rows of color B to 111 sts, ending with a WS row, and a full stripe of color A.
Rows 111–120: With color B, BO 1 st at the beg of every row, k to end—101 sts.

Rem rows of Center Panel: Change to color A. Work the remainder of the center panel as established in Rows 111–120, dec 1 st at the beg of every row, and continuing to alternate 10 rows of color A with 10 rows of color B, until 1 st rem. Cut yarn and fasten off rem stitch.

Border

The remainder of the blanket is made up of garter and St st bands and is worked in the round. To do this you will pick up stitches along the four sides of the center panel, including 1 st for each corner, and work around all four sides of the panel. On every other round, you will inc before and after each corner stitch.

First Garter Stitch Band

Beg at a corner of the blanket and with RS facing, use color C and 40" needle to *pick up 81 sts evenly along one side of the blanket, pm, pickup 1 corner stitch, pm, rotate work clockwise. Rep from * around all four sides of the center panel, ending at the corner where you began—328 sts. Place the contrasting marker and join work in the round.

Rnd 1: *P to marker, sm, k1, sm; rep from * to end.
Rnd 2: M1, *k to marker, M1, sm, k1, sm, M1; rep from * twice more, k to marker, M1, sm, k1, sm (8 sts increased)—336 sts.
Rnd 3: Purl, slipping markers as you go.
Rnds 4–7: Rep Rnds 2 and 3—352 sts.

Stockinette Band and Star Motif

The first and last 2 rounds of this band are worked in color A. After knitting the first two rounds of this band, you will work the star motif using the chart below. The chart is worked using the Fair Isle technique in colors D and E, with color A as the background. To work the patt motif, read the chart from the bottom up, and from right to left on all rounds.

NOTE: When working Fair Isle always bring the new color *under* the one last used. This creates a twist, locking the yarn in place and prevents a hole from forming at the color changes.

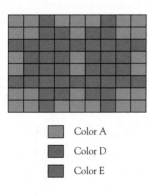

Color A
Color D
Color E

Begin Band
Join color A. M1, *k to marker, M1, sm, k1, sm, M1; rep from * twice more, k to marker, M1, sm, k1, sm—360 sts.
Next Rnd: Knit.

Work Star Motif
There are seven repeats of the chart on each side of the blanket with 4 sts worked in between. Use color A for the background stitches of the chart and for the 4 sts between each chart repeat.

Rnd 1: *M1, k1 in color A, (work Row 1 of chart, k4 sts in color A) 6 times, work Row 1 of chart, k1 in color A, M1, sm, k corner stitch in color A, sm; rep from * around to contrasting marker—368 sts.
Rnd 2: Knit, working Row 2 of chart at the intervals established in Row 1.
Rnds 3–8: Work rem rows of chart as established, inc 8 sts every other round (2 sts at each corner) as indicated in Rnd 1—392 sts.
Cut contrast colors D and E.

Finish Stockinette Stitch Band
Working in color A only, M1, *k to marker, M1, sm, k1, sm, M1; rep from * twice more, k to marker, M1, sm, k1, sm—400 sts.

Last rnd of band: Knit. Cut color A.

Second Garter Stitch Band
Join color C.
Rnd 1: M1, *k to marker, M1, sm, k1, sm, M1; rep from * twice more, k to marker, M1, sm, k1, sm (8 sts increased)—408 sts.
Rnd 2: *P to marker, sm, k1, sm; rep from * around.
Rnds 3–8: Rep rnds 1 and 2. End with 107 sts between markers plus 4 corner sts—432 sts total.

Cut yarn. Do not BO stitches. The triangle trim is worked with the live stitches of the blanket edge.

Triangle Trim
The triangle trim is worked back and forth in rows around the edge of the blanket. Each triangle is worked one at a time and is finished and fastened off before beg the next triangle. The base of each triangle is worked across 18 sts from the blanket edge. There are six triangles per side. The color patt for the triangle trim repeats around the sides of the blanket using colors E, B, and D (see photos).

Triangles 1 and 4
Rows 1 and 2: With color E, knit the first 18 sts of the round, turn.
Row 3 (RS): Ssk, k16, turn.

Rows 4–18: Continue as in Row 3, dec 1 st at the beg of every row until 2 sts rem.

Row 19: Ssk—1 st rem. To finish the triangle, cut the yarn and pull the tail through the rem st.

Triangles 2 and 5

With RS facing, join color B and working over the next 18 sts of the round, make the second triangle by rep Rows 1–19.

Triangles 3 and 6

With RS facing, join color D and rep Rows 1–19 (as above) over the next 18 sts.

Continue in this way across all of the stitches on one side of the blanket. The 18th stitch of the last triangle on each side will be a corner stitch. Rotate the blanket clockwise, just as if you were knitting in the round, and rep for the second, third, and fourth sides of the blanket.

French Knots

French knots are used to embellish the two garter stitch bands of the blanket border. With color B and a tapestry needle, embroider a line of French knots in the ditch formed between the second and third ridges of the first garter stitch band. Space the French knots so that there are about 3 sts between each knot. Continue stitching French knots around all four sides of the blanket. Rep for the second garter stitch band.

Pompoms

Make 24 pompoms, 12 each of color A and color C, as per instructions on page 155.

Finishing

Weave in all ends. Block blanket. Sew pompoms to triangle trim alternating color A and color C.

Pirates

vast, me hardies, it's time for adventure on the high seas! This group of patterns includes a little something for the whole crew—a felted bag for toting treasure, a stripey sweater for your first mate, a dress for your favorite pirate lass, and hats to match. Whether they are swabbing the decks or trimming the sails, your shipmates will cut a fine figure in these outfits.

Sweater

This sweater is just the thing for your favorite cabin boy or girl. Knotted seed stitch tabs give this sweater a nautical look that is sure to please any youngster yearning for the thrill of pirate life.

Stripey Hat

Your shipmates will love this stripey hat. It looks great on pirates, young and old, and can be worn two ways—short, with the ties tied tight, or loose and slouchy.

Messenger Bag

After a day of swashbuckling fun, your crew can transport their kit in this pirate bag. Favored by buccaneers of all ages, this roomy bag is made of dense felt and is great for carrying school books as well as treasure.

Dress

Perfect for pirating all year long, this adorable outfit can be worn as a sundress for summer and as a jumper for spring, winter, and fall. It is ideal for everything from dining at the captain's table to searching for buried treasure. Versatile and easy to wear, this pretty dress is what every pirate lass needs.

Lass Hat

With its seed stitch hatband and pretty bow tie, this little hat has loads of personality and charm. Comfortable and cute, this hat will be a favorite for years to come.

Sweater

This sweater is worked from the bottom up, beginning with the lower border, which is made of rectangular seed stitch tabs. Each tab is worked back and forth in rows. Once all of the tabs are complete, they are joined together and the work progresses in the round. The body of the sweater is worked in stockinette rounds up to the armholes where the sweater is divided for front and back, and worked back and forth in rows. The shoulder seams are joined with a three-needle bind-off, and the sleeves are knitted in the round from armhole to cuff.

SIZES
12–24 months (4 years, 6 years, 8 years)

FINISHED MEASUREMENTS
Chest: 26 (29, 32, 35)" [66 (74, 81, 89)cm]
Shoulder to hem: 13 (14$^1/_2$, 15$^1/_2$, 17$^1/_2$)" [33 (37, 39, 44)cm]

Sample size 8 years

MATERIALS
Tahki/Stacy Charles *Cotton Classic* (100% mercerized cotton; 108 yd. [100m] per 50g skein): #3002 Black (color A), 5 (5, 6, 6) skeins; #3001 White (color B), 3 (3, 4, 4) skeins
US 5 (3.75mm) 24" circular needle
US 5 (3.75mm) 16" circular needle
US 5 (3.75mm) double-pointed needles
US 4 (3.5mm) 16" circular needle
US 4 (3.5mm) double-pointed needles
Stitch holder or scrap yarn
Stitch markers
Row counter
Tapestry needle

GAUGE
20 sts and 26 rows = 4" (10cm) in St st on US 5 (3.75mm) needle, or size needed to obtain gauge

STITCH PATTERNS
Stockinette stitch worked in the round—Knit every round.
Stockinette stitch worked flat—Knit one row; purl one row.
Seed stitch worked flat or in the round—On first row or round, *k1, p1; rep from * to end. On subsequent rows or rounds, purl the knits and knit the purls.
K2tog (page 149)
P2tog (page 150)
Ssk (page 150)
Ssp (page 150)

SPECIAL TECHNIQUES
Three-needle bind-off (page 151)

Instructions

Border

The border is made up of 16 (18, 20, 22) seed stitch tabs, which are worked separately and then knitted together. You can work the border on the 16" US 4 needle, pushing each tab down the needle as you begin the next one, or you can work the tabs on US 4 dpns, slipping each one to the circular needle as it's completed.

With color A and a US 4 needle, CO 8 sts.
Row 1 (RS): *K1, p1; rep from * to end.
Row 2: *P1, k1; rep from * to end.
Rep Rows 1 and 2 until work measures 5" (13cm), ending with a WS row.

Cut yarn, leaving a long tail for weaving in later. Make 16 (18, 20, 22) tabs.

Do not cut the yarn after making the last tab. Place all of the tabs on the 16" needle with the tail of each tab trailing from the right hand side, so that you are ready to begin a RS row.

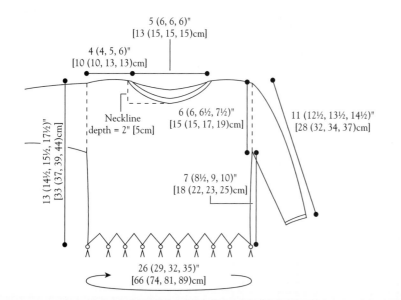

5 (6, 6, 6)"
[13 (15, 15, 15)cm]

4 (4, 5, 6)"
[10 (10, 13, 13)cm]

Neckline depth = 2" [5cm]

6 (6, 6½, 7½)"
[15 (15, 17, 19)cm]

11 (12½, 13½, 14½)"
[28 (32, 34, 37)cm]

13 (14½, 15½, 17½)"
[33 (37, 39, 44)cm]

7 (8½, 9, 10)"
[18 (22, 23, 25)cm]

26 (29, 32, 35)"
[66 (74, 81, 89)cm]

Join border tabs

(RS): *K1, p1; rep from * across 8 (9, 10, 11) of the tabs [64 (72, 80, 88) sts], pm, rep from * across the remaining 8 (9, 10, 11) tabs and place a contrasting marker to mark the beg of the round. Join work in the round, taking care not to twist stitches—128 (144, 160, 176) sts.

Sweater Body

Switch to 24" US 5 needle.

NOTE: At the beginning of the second round of each stripe (Rnds 2 and 9 for the sweater body and Rnds 2 and 6 for the sleeves) use the tip of the right needle to pick up the stitch below the first stitch on the left needle. Place this stitch on the end of the left needle and knit it together with the first stitch of this round. This technique applies to knitting in the round only and is optional, but eliminates the color jog that occurs when working stripes in the round.

Rnds 1–7: Knit color A. Cut yarn.
Rnds 8–14: Knit color B. Cut yarn.

Continue in St st stripe patt as established in Rnds 1–14, alternating stripes, until piece measures 7 (8½, 9, 10)" [18 (22, 23, 25)cm] from joined edge.

Divide for Front and Back

At this point, the work will be divided for the front and back of the sweater, and the sweater will be worked back and forth in rows. You will continue to work in established stripe patt for the remainder of the sweater body.

With RS facing, k64 (72, 80, 88) sts for sweater back, turn, and purl back to beg of round. Put rem 64 (72, 80, 88) sts on a holder or spare needle for sweater front, which will be worked later.

Back

Work sweater back in St st stripe patt, until piece measures 13 (14½, 15½, 17½)" [33 (37, 39, 44)cm] from joined edge of border, ending with a WS row. Make a note of the number of rows worked so that you can rep the same number on the front. Cut yarn. Place the stitches for the sweater back on a holder or spare needle where they will be held in reserve while you work the front of the sweater.

Front

Slide the stitches on reserve for sweater front onto the 24" US 5 needle. Join new skein of yarn (the color needed to maintain the stripe patt) and beg at left underarm with RS facing.

Next row (RS): K64 (72, 80, 88) sts.
Work in St st, as for sweater back, maintaining stripe patt until front measures 11 (12½,13½, 15½)" [28 (32, 34, 39)cm] from the joined edge of the border, ending with a WS row.

Front Neckline Shaping

The shaping for the right and left sides of the front neckline is worked simultaneously. After working across the left shoulder, a second skein of yarn is introduced for the center neck and the right shoulder. On each row you will work one shoulder with one skein and the other shoulder with the second skein. You can work the shoulders on two separate dpns or use the same circular for both shoulders.

While working on the neckline shaping, continue in St st maintaining the stripe patt on both shoulders.

Row 1 (RS): Beg at the left armhole, k27 (30, 33, 37) sts, join new yarn, BO center 10 (12, 14, 14) sts for center neck, k rem 27 (30, 33, 37) sts for right shoulder.

Row 2: P27 (30, 33, 37) for right shoulder, drop yarn for right shoulder, skip over the stitches for the center neck, pick up yarn for left shoulder and BO 3 sts (pwise) at left neck edge, p to end. You will continue in this manner for the remainder of the neckline, working one shoulder from the armhole edge to the neck opening, skipping over the center stitches and then working the other shoulder from the neck opening to the armhole.

Row 3: K24 (27, 30, 34) for left shoulder. Beg at right neck edge, BO 3 sts (kwise), k to end.

Row 4: P24 (27, 30, 34) for right shoulder. Beg at left neck edge BO 2 sts (pwise), p to end.

Row 5: K22 (25, 28, 32) for left shoulder. Beg at right neck edge, BO 2 sts (kwise), k to end.

Row 6: Beg at right armhole, p19 (22, 25, 29), p2tog, p1, end at right neck edge. Beg at left neck edge, p1, ssp, p19 (22, 25, 29) to left armhole.

Row 7: Beg at left armhole, k18 (21, 24, 28), k2tog, k1, end at left neck edge. Beg at right neck edge, k1, ssk, k18 (21, 24, 28) to right armhole.

Row 8: Beg at right armhole, p17 (20, 23, 27), p2tog, p1, end at right neck edge. Beg at left neck edge, p1 ssp, p17 (20, 23, 27).

At the end of the neckline shaping, 19 (22, 25, 29) sts rem for each shoulder.

Continue in St st, working both shoulders without further shaping until front measures 13 (14½, 15½, 17½)" [33 (37, 39, 44)cm] from joined edge of border (same number of rows as for sweater back), ending with a WS row. Cut yarn.

Shoulder Seams

Transfer each set of 19 (22, 25, 29) shoulder sts for the left back and left front shoulder each onto a separate US 5 dpn. Rep for the right shoulder. Place the 26 (28, 30, 30) sts for center back on a holder to be worked later. Turn the sweater inside out so that the RS of the sweater are together.

Work the shoulder seams with the same color of yarn used to make the last stripe. With WS facing and beg at the right armhole edge, join the front and back right shoulder stitches together with a three-needle bind-off. Cut yarn and fasten off.

Leave the center stitches for the back of the neck on the holder for later.

Rep for left shoulder seam, working from the armhole to the neck edge.

Sleeves

The stripe patt for the sleeves is different from that of the sweater. The sleeves are worked in St st in a four-round stripe patt (4 rounds color A, 4 rounds color B). As you work the stripe patt, you will shape the sleeves at the same time, working decrease rounds as you go.

Using US 4 dpns, color A, and beg at base of left armhole with RS facing, pick up 62 (68, 72, 78) sts around armhole edge. Arrange the stitches evenly on the dpns, pm, and join in a round.

Begin working stripe patt, switching to US 5 double point needles after first round.

At the same time, shape sleeves by decreasing 2 sts (see Dec Rnd below) every sixth round 1 (2, 4, 6) times to 60 (64, 64, 66) sts, and every fourth round 13 (14, 13, 12) times to 34 (36, 38, 42) sts.

Dec Rnd: K1, ssk, k to within 3 sts of marker, k2tog, k1.

Work without further shaping until sleeve measures approximately 10 (11, 12½, 13½)" [25 (28, 32, 34)cm]. You may begin the cuff at this point, regardless of whether you have completed a full stripe. If you wish to end the sleeve with a full stripe, you will make 16 (18, 20, 22) stripes total, ending with color B.

Cuff

Change to US 4 dpns, and work cuff in color A.
Rnd 1: Knit.
Rnds 2, 4, and 6: *K1, p1; rep from * to end.
Rnds 3, 5, and 7: *P1, k1; rep from * to end.
BO all stitches kwise. Cut yarn and fasten off.

Repeat for right sleeve.

Neckband

Beg at back right shoulder with RS facing and using 16"
US 4 needle or US 4 dpns, join color A and knit across the
26 (28, 30, 30) sts on hold for the back neckline, pick up
44 (46, 48, 50) sts evenly around the front neckline edge,
ending at the right shoulder where you began—70 (74, 78,
80) sts.

Place a marker and join in the round.
Rnd 1: *K1, p1; rep from * to end.
Rnd 2: *P1, k1; rep from * to end.

Rep Rnds 1 and 2 twice more. BO kwise. Cut yarn and
fasten off.

Finishing

Weave in all ends. Block sweater. Tie a knot in each of the
border tabs.

Stripey Hat

This hat is worked in the round from the bottom edge up.
At the top of the hat, the stitches are divided and the ties
are worked one at a time in the round.

SIZES
6–12 months (2–4 years, 4–6 years, 6–8 years)

FINISHED MEASUREMENTS
Head circumference: 15 (17, 19, 21)" [38 (43, 48, 53)cm]

Sample size 2–4 years

MATERIALS
Tahki/Stacy Charles *Cotton Classic* (100% mercerized cotton; 108 yd.
  [100m] per 50g skein): #3002 Black (color A), 1 (1, 1, 1) skein;
  #3001 White (color B), 1 (1, 1, 1) skein
US 5 (3.75mm) 12" circular needle (for 6–12 month size only)
US 5 (3.75mm) 16" circular needle (for all other sizes)
US 5 (3.75mm) double-pointed needles
US 3 (3.25mm) 12" circular needle (for 6–12 month size only)
US 3 (3.25mm) 16" circular needle (for all other sizes)
Stitch markers
Row counter
Stitch holders
Tapestry needle
Safety pin
Sewing needle and thread to match yarn (optional)

GAUGE

20 sts and 26 rows = 4" (10cm) in St st on US 5 (3.75mm) needle, or size needed to obtain gauge

STITCH PATTERNS

Stockinette stitch worked in the round—Knit all stitches every round.

Seed stitch worked in the round—On first round, *k1, p1; rep from * to end. On subsequent rounds, purl the knits and knit the purls.

K2tog (page 149)

SPECIAL TECHNIQUES

Three-needle bind-off (page 151)

Instructions

Hatband

With US 3 circular needle and color A, CO 74 (84, 96, 106) sts, pm, and join work in the round.

Rnds 1, 3, and 5: *K1, p1; rep from * to end.
Rnds 2, 4, and 6: *P1, k1; rep from * to end.

Stripe Pattern

Switch to US 5 needle and color B. Do not cut color A.

Join yarn at beg of each stripe by dropping the color from the last stripe; do not cut it. To begin each stripe, bring the new color up and to the left of the dropped yarn. Rep this for each new stripe, running the yarn up the side of the hat and locking it in place.

NOTE: Here is a handy trick for hiding the color jog that occurs at the beginning of each new stripe. At the beginning of Rnds 2 and 6 use the tip of the right needle to pick up the stitch below the first stitch on the left needle. Place this stitch on the end of the left needle and knit it together with the first stitch of the round.

Rnds 1–4: Knit color B.
Rnds 5–8: Knit color A.

Continue in stripe patt until you have a total of 40 (44, 48, 52) rounds [10 (11, 12, 13) stripes in all, not including hatband].

Knit the first round of next stripe.

Hat Ties

Keep the stripe patt going as you work the ties. You will work one tie first (in the round with dpns), leaving the rem stitches on the circular needle. After the first tie is complete, a second skein of yarn is joined for the center seam. A three-needle bind-off worked across the center stitches closes the top of the hat. The second tie is worked in the round with the rem stitches.

First Tie

With US 5 dpns, k20 (20, 24, 24) sts for the first hat tie. Leave rem 54 (64, 72, 82) sts on the circular needle to be worked later. Mark the first stitch on the circular needle with a safety pin. This will indicate where to begin dividing stitches for the center seam later in the pattern. At this point you will beg working on the first tie. You will work on the stitches for this tie only until it has been completed. Divide the 20 (20, 24, 24) sts on three dpns, pm, and join in the round.

NOTE: The first couple of rounds may feel a bit awkward, but after you have completed them the knitting progresses quickly and smoothly.

Continue, knitting stripe patt in St st, working in the round on the stitches of the first tie only, until you have 7 (7, 8, 8) stripes.

Tie Shaping

Rnd 1: *K2tog; rep from * to end—10 (10, 12, 12) sts.
Rnds 2 and 4: Knit.
Rnd 3: *K2tog; rep from * to end—5 (5, 6, 6) sts.

Cut the yarn leaving a 12" (30cm) tail. Thread a tapestry needle with the tail of the tie and run the needle through the rem stitches to close the top. Pull taut and insert the needle into the fabric to the inside of tie, secure with a small stitch, and fasten off.

Center Seam

To make the center seam and the second tie, you will need to rearrange stitches rem on the circular needle. Beg with the first stitch on the circular needle (the stitch you marked with the safety pin) and RS facing, divide the rem 54 (64, 72, 82) sts on the circular needle evenly onto two US 5 dpns. Arrange the dpns so that they are parallel to one another and so that the stitch marked with the safety pin is the first stitch on the dpn closest to you. With WS of work together, join yarn for the center seam, leaving a long tail and using the same color that you used for the first round of the first tie. Remove the safety pin and work a three-needle bind-off across the center 17 (22, 24, 29) sts. Cut yarn and fasten off.

Join yarn for the second tie, leaving a long tail and using the same color that you used for the center seam. Using dpns, knit across the rem 20 (20, 24, 24) sts. Arrange the stitches on three dpns, pm, and join work in the round.

Second Tie

Work second tie as you did the first, maintaining stripe patt and shaping the top of the tie in the same manner.

Finishing

Thread a tapestry needle with the tail from the beginning of the center seam. Working with RS facing, stitch together the little hole that may have formed between the first tie and the center seam. Weave in end and trim tail. Rep for second tie.
Weave in rem ends. Block hat.
Tie the top ties of the hat together. Secure the position of the tie by stitching through it and the hat with needle and thread, if desired.

Messenger Bag

This seamless messenger bag is worked from the bottom up, with both flat and circular knitting techniques. To make this bag, you will first knit a striped garter stitch rectangle. This is the base of the bag, and it is worked back and forth in rows. After the base is complete, stitches are picked up around the edges of the rectangle, and the body of the bag is worked in the round. Once the body of the bag is complete, stitches for the front and two short sides are bound off and the flap is worked back and forth in rows with the remaining stitches. The flap is embellished with intarsia colorwork, but if you prefer you could work the flap as a solid color and add the pattern motif in duplicate stitch (before felting). The strap is worked separately, in garter stitch. After the bag and strap are completed, they are felted in the washer. The strap is sewn to the bag after blocking.

FINISHED MEASUREMENTS
Before Felting
Height: 17" (43cm)
Base: 21" × 6" (53cm × 15cm)

After Felting
Height: 11$^1/_2$" (29cm)
Base: 14$^1/_2$" × 4$^1/_2$" (37cm × 11cm)

NOTE: The finished size of your bag may vary, depending on the degree of felting. The finished measurements here reflect a densely felted fabric.

MATERIALS

Cascade Yarns *220* (100% Peruvian Highland Wool; 220 yd. [201m] per 100 g skein): #8555 Black (color A), 6 skeins; #9491 Charcoal (color B), 2 skeins.
US 11 (8mm) 24" circular needle
US 11 (8mm) 32" circular needle
US 11 (8mm) double-pointed needles
Bobbins (optional)
Row counter
Stitch markers
Tapestry needle
Upholstery thread or embroidery floss to match bag
Sewing needle
Sewing thread to match yarn

GAUGE (BEFORE FELTING)

11 sts and 15 rows = 4" (10cm) with yarn held double in St st on US 11 needle, or size needed to obtain gauge

NOTE: If you decide to use different yarn to make this bag, look for 100% wool yarn that, by itself, has a gauge of 18–20 sts per 4" (10cm) in St st on US 7–8 (4.5–5mm) needles.

STITCH PATTERNS

Stockinette stitch worked flat—Knit on RS rows; purl on WS rows.
Stockinette stitch worked in the round—Knit all stitches every round.
Garter stitch worked in the round—Knit one round, purl one round.
Garter stitch worked flat—Knit all stitches every row.
K2tog (page 149)
Ssk (page 150)

SPECIAL TECHNIQUES

Intarsia (page 157)
Three-needle bind-off (page 151)
Felting (page 160)
Duplicate stitch (page 157)

Instructions

NOTE: The yarn is double-stranded throughout this project (two strands held together as one).

Bag Base

With double strand of color A and 24" needle, CO 48 sts.
Rows 1 and 2: Knit color A.

Rows 3 and 4: Knit color B.
Rows 5–16: Rep Rows 1–4 three more times.
Rows 17–19: Knit color A. Do not turn work after Row 19.

In the following steps, you will pick up stitches along the three other sides of the rectangle.

With all the stitches from Row 19 on the RH needle and the working yarn trailing off the left side of the work, pm on end of the RH needle and rotate the piece to the right. Pick up 12 sts evenly along the short side of the piece adjacent to the corner where the last stitch of Row 19 was knitted. Place the second marker at this corner, rotate work to the right, and pick up 48 sts evenly on the long side of the piece. Place the third marker at this corner, rotate work, and pick up 12 sts on rem short side of the rectangle—120 sts. Place a contrasting marker at the fourth corner.

Bag Body

The body of the bag is worked in the round with color A. The contrasting marker indicates beg of the round.

Rnd 1 is a preparatory round. Rnds 2–4 form the turning ridge around the base of the bag.
Rnd 1: With 32" needle, k48, sm, p rem 72 sts, slipping markers as you go.
Rnds 2–4: Purl.
Rnd 5: Knit.
Rnd 6: K48, sm, p12, sm, k48, sm, p12, sm.
Rnds 5 and 6 form the patt for the body of the bag. The front and back of the bag are worked in St st (knit every round) and the sides of the bag are worked in garter stitch (knit one round, purl one round).
Rnds 7–58: Rep Rnds 5 and 6.
Rnd 59: K48, sm, ssk, k8, k2tog, sm, k48, sm, ssk, k8, k2tog, sm—116 sts.
Rnds 60, 62, and 64: Purl.
Rnds 61 and 63: Knit.
Rnd 65: K48 (these stitches form the flap), BO all rem stitches, discarding the markers as you go. Do not cut yarn. Fasten off the last bound-off stitch by bringing the skein of working yarn through the loop on the RH needle. To make the loop big enough to accommodate the skein of yarn, take the loop off of the needle and open it up by gently

pulling on it. Pass the skein of yarn through the loop and then pull on the tail of the yarn to tighten and fasten off the stitch. You will continue to use this yarn to work the flap of the bag.

After working Rnd 65, you will end at the back of the bag with the RS facing. The 48 live sts for the flap will be on the LH needle.

Flap

The flap of the bag is worked back and forth in rows from the top edge of the bag down to the final edge of the flap. To avoid curling along the sides of the flap, the first and last 4 sts of the flap are worked in garter stitch. The center 40 sts are worked in St st throughout.

Row 1 (RS): K4, pm, k40, pm, k4, turn work—48 sts.
Row 2 (WS): K4, sm, p40, sm, K4—48 sts.
Rows 3–17: Continue working as established in Rows 1 and 2.
Row 18 (WS): K4, sm, p5, place contrasting marker, p30, place contrasting marker, p5, sm, k4.

The contrasting markers indicate the placement of the patt chart. The 30 sts of the patt chart are centered between these two markers.

As you work the remainder of the flap, continue to knit the first and last 4 sts of each row (garter stitch). All other stitches of the flap are worked in St st.

Work Chart

The chart for this pattern is worked in St st, from the bottom up. Read the chart from right to left on RS rows, knitting all stitches, and from left to right on all WS rows, purling across. The background stitches of the chart and all other flap stitches are worked with color A.

NOTE: Because you do not carry the yarn across the back of the work when changing colors in intarsia, you will need to twist the yarns together to prevent a hole from forming where the color change occurs. To do this on RS rows, pick up the new yarn from underneath the yarn just used. On WS rows, drop the yarn just used and bring the new yarn up and to the right of the yarn just used to twist the yarns.

Prepare to work the patt motif by winding several bobbins (double stranded) of colors A and B. You will need separate balls of color A for the sides around the intarsia motif as well.

Row 1 (RS): Continuing with color A, k4, sm, k5, sm, knit across chart stitches beg with Row 1 using color B for the patt motif and color A for the background, sm, with color A, k5, sm, k4.
Row 2 (WS): With color A, k4, sm, p5, sm, purl across chart stitches beg with Row 2, using color B for the patt motif and color A for the background, sm, with color A, p5, sm, k4.
Rows 3–40: Continue working charted section of flap as established, ending with a WS row. Cut color B.

End Flap

With RS of flap facing: K48 color A.
Next row (WS): K4, p40, k4.
Knit the next four rows in garter stitch. Do not cut yarn.

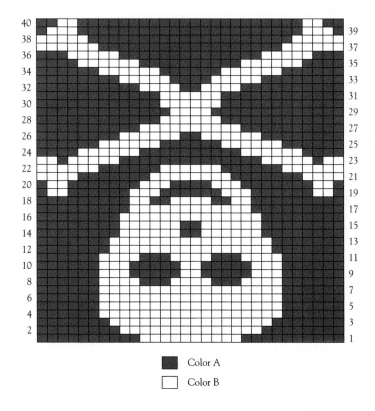

Color A
Color B

Flap Edging

There are four triangular points decorating the bottom edge of the flap. Each point is made one at a time by working across 12 sts from the flap. To begin the first point, you will work across the first 12 sts of the flap while leaving the rem 36 sts held in reserve on the 32" needle. To make each point, work through Row 10 and fasten off the completed point. Beg the next point by joining the yarn, with the RS of the flap facing, and working Rows 1–10 with the next 12 sts of the flap. Continue in this manner until all of the flap stitches have been worked.

Row 1 (RS): With dpns, k1, ssk, k6, k2tog, k1, turn—10 sts.
Rows 2, 4, 6, and 8: Knit.
Row 3: K1, ssk, k4, k2tog, k1, turn—8 sts.
Row 5: K1, ssk, k2, k2tog, k1, turn—6 sts.
Row 7: K1, ssk, k2tog, k1, turn—4 sts.
Row 9: Ssk, k2tog, turn—2 sts.
Row 10: K2tog, cut yarn and fasten off.

First point completed. With RS facing, join double strand of color A for the next point and rep Rows 1–10 with the next group of 12 sts.

Handle

With dpns and two strands of color A, CO 10 sts. Knit every row for 38" (97cm). BO.

NOTE: A purchased handle would also work well for this bag. Many fabric stores have nylon webbing purse and bag handles with adjustable lengths. This is a nice alternative for active and growing kids.

Finishing

Weave in all ends. Felt and block bag and handle as per instructions on page 160.
Sew the handle to the upper-right and left sides of the bag.

Dress

This dress is made with both circular and flat knitting and is worked from the hem up. The striped skirt is worked in the round in stockinette stitch and is gathered with a decrease round at the bodice edge. The bodice is worked in the round in seed stitch up to the armholes where the work is divided for the front and the back of the dress. The remainder of the dress bodice is worked back and forth in rows. A three-needle bind-off joins the shoulder seams and crochet trim along the neck and armhole edges finishes the dress.

SIZES
6–12 months (2 years, 3 years, 4 years, 5 years)

FINISHED MEASUREMENTS
Chest: 18 (20, 22, 24, 26)" [46 (51, 56, 61, 66)cm]
Shoulder to hem: $16^1/_2$ (19, 21, $23^1/_2$, 26)" [42 (48, 53, 60, 66)cm]

Sample size 6–12 months

MATERIALS
Tahki/Stacy Charles *Cotton Classic* (100% mercerized cotton; 108 yd. [100m] per 50g skein): #3002 Black (color A), 3 (4, 4, 5, 6) skeins; #3001 White (color B), 2 (3, 3, 4, 5) skeins
US 3 (3.25mm) 16" circular needle
US 3 (3.25mm) 24" circular needle
US 3 (3.25 mm) double-pointed needles
US 5 (3.75mm) 24" circular needle
US size D (3.25mm) crochet hook
Stitch holder
Stitch markers
Row counter
Tapestry needle

GAUGE
20 sts and 26 rows = 4" (10cm) in St st on US 5 (3.75mm) needle, or size needed to obtain gauge
20 sts and 36 rows = 4" (10cm) in seed stitch on US 3 (3.25mm) needle, or size needed to obtain gauge

STITCH PATTERNS
Seed stitch worked flat or in the round—On first row or round, *k1, p1; rep from * to end. On subsequent rows or rounds, purl the knits and knit the purls.
Stockinette stitch worked in the round—Knit all stitches every round.
K2tog (page 149)
Ssk (page 150)

round, being careful not to twist stitches—180 (200, 220, 240, 260) sts.

Rnd 1: *K1, p1; rep from * to end.
Rnd 2: *P1, k1; rep from * to end.
Repeat Rnds 1 and 2 twice.
Do not cut yarn.

Skirt
Switch to 24" US 5 needle to work the skirt. Join color B to work first stripe.

Stripe Pattern
Work each new stripe by dropping the color from the last stripe; do not cut yarn. To beg each new stripe, bring the new color up and to the left of the dropped yarn. Rep this for each new stripe, running the yarn up the side of the skirt.

NOTE: At the beginning of Rnds 2 and 8 use the tip of the right needle to pick up the stitch below the first stitch on the left needle. Place this stitch on the end of the left needle and knit it together with the first stitch of the round. Doing this is optional, but it corrects the color jog that occurs at the beginning of each new stripe.

Rnds 1–6: Knit, using color B.
Rnds 7–12: Knit, using color A.

Continue in St st in stripe patt until skirt measures approximately 10½ (12, 13½, 15, 17)" [27 (30, 34, 38, 43) cm] from CO edge.
Cut yarn.

Gather Skirt
With US 3 needle and color A (use 16" needle for sizes 6 months–3 years, and 24" needle for sizes 4–5 years).
K2tog around, keeping markers in place—90 (100, 110, 120 130) sts.

Bodice
Continuing to use US 3 needle, work bodice in seed stitch in color A.
Rnd 1: *K1, p1; rep from * to end, slipping the markers as you go.

SPECIAL TECHNIQUES
Three-needle bind-off (page 151)
Crochet picot trim (see the instructions in this pattern)

Instructions
Dress Skirt
Seed Stitch Border
With 24" US 3 needle and color A, CO 90 (100, 110, 120, 130) sts, pm, CO 90 (100, 110, 120, 130) sts, place a contrasting marker to mark beg of the round. Join in the

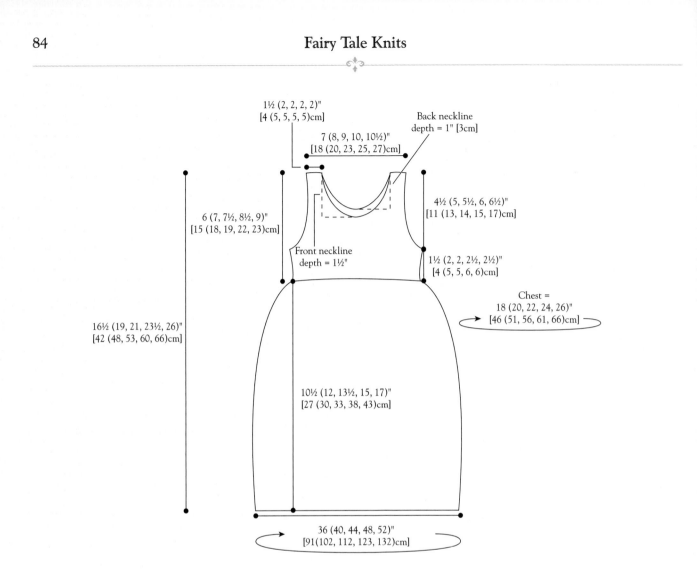

1½ (2, 2, 2, 2)"
[4 (5, 5, 5, 5)cm]

Back neckline
depth = 1" [3cm]

7 (8, 9, 10, 10½)"
[18 (20, 23, 25, 27)cm]

4½ (5, 5½, 6, 6½)"
[11 (13, 14, 15, 17)cm]

6 (7, 7½, 8½, 9)"
[15 (18, 19, 22, 23)cm]

Front neckline
depth = 1½"

1½ (2, 2, 2½, 2½)"
[4 (5, 5, 6, 6)cm]

Chest =
18 (20, 22, 24, 26)"
[46 (51, 56, 61, 66)cm]

16½ (19, 21, 23½, 26)"
[42 (48, 53, 60, 66)cm]

10½ (12, 13½, 15, 17)"
[27 (30, 33, 38, 43)cm]

36 (40, 44, 48, 52)"
[91(102, 112, 123, 132)cm]

Rnd 2: *P1, k1; rep from * to end, slipping the markers as you go.

Rep last two rows until bodice measures 1½ (2, 2, 2½, 2½)" [4 (5, 5, 6, 6)cm].

Divide for Front and Back

At this point the bodice will be divided for the front and back of the dress. You will be working back and forth in rows for the rem of the bodice.

Bodice Back
Armhole Shaping

Row 1 (RS): BO 2 sts in patt for right underarm, work in seed stitch to first marker—43 (48, 53, 58, 63) sts. Place rem 45 (50, 55, 60, 65) sts on a holder or spare needle for bodice front, which will be worked later. Turn work and continue to work on the stitches for the bodice back only.

Row 2 (WS): BO 2 sts in patt for left underarm, work in seed stitch to end of row—41 (46, 51, 56, 61) sts.

Row 3: Ssk at right armhole edge, work in seed stitch to last 2 sts, k2tog at left armhole edge—39 (44, 49, 54, 59) sts.

Row 4: Work in seed stitch.

Rep last two rows 1 (2, 2, 2, 3) time(s)—37 (40, 45, 50, 53) sts.

Continue to work in seed stitch without shaping until the bodice measures 3½ (4, 4½, 5, 5½)" [9 (10, 11, 13, 14)cm], ending with a WS row.

Neckline Shaping

The left and right neckline edges are worked in tandem. To begin the neckline shaping, you will work across the stitches for one shoulder, drop the yarn you've been using (don't cut it), join a second skein of yarn, BO stitches for the center neck, and work the second shoulder. You will be using two skeins of yarn, one for each shoulder. On each row, you will be working from the armhole to the neck edge for the first shoulder, and from the neck to the armhole edge for the second shoulder.

Row 1 (RS): Work seed stitch over first 14 (15, 17, 19, 20) sts for the right shoulder. Join a second skein of yarn and BO center 9 (10, 11, 12, 13) sts for the back of the neck. Work rem 14 (15, 17, 19, 20) sts in seed stitch for the left shoulder.
Row 2 (WS): Work in seed stitch across each shoulder.
Row 3: Work in patt to last 2 sts of right shoulder, k2tog at neck edge. Move to left shoulder, ssk at neck edge, work in patt to end of row—13 (14, 16, 18, 19) sts for each strap.
Row 4: Rep Row 2.
Rep last two rows 5 (5, 6, 7, 7) times—8 (9, 10, 11, 12) sts each side.

Continue working on the rem shoulder stitches without further shaping until the bodice measures 6 (7, 7½, 8½, 9)" [15 (18, 19, 22, 23)cm], ending with a WS row. Put each set of shoulder stitches on a holder or US 3 dpn to be held in reserve for later. Cut yarn.

Bodice Front

Slide the 45 (50, 55, 60, 65) sts on reserve for bodice front onto 16" or 24" US 3 needle. Beg at left armhole with RS facing, join color A and work bodice front as for back through the armhole shaping —37 (40, 45, 50, 53) sts. After the armhole shaping is complete, continue working in seed stitch without shaping until bodice measures 3 (3½, 4, 4½, 5)" [8 (9, 10, 11, 13)cm].

Work front neckline shaping as for back, dec at neck edge until 8 (9, 10, 11, 12) sts rem. Continue to work without shaping until front measures the same as back, ending with a WS row.

Shoulder Seams

Put each set of shoulder stitches on a separate US 3 dpn. Turn the dress inside out so that the RS of the dress are together. Beg at the left armhole edge, with WS of work and the back of the dress facing you, join color A. Holding the dpns parallel to one another, work a three-needle bind-off across the left shoulder. Cut yarn and fasten off.

Arrange work so that the front of the dress is facing you. Beg at right armhole edge, with WS facing, rep for right shoulder seam.

Crochet Picot Trim

The armhole and neckline edges are trimmed with a crocheted picot trim. Work picot trim around neckline, beg and ending at the center back.

With RS facing, crochet hook, and color B, crochet into an edge stitch by holding the yarn at the back of work and inserting the hook into the fabric from the RS to the WS of work. Wrap a loop of the working yarn around the hook and pull the loop up from the WS through the stitch and to the RS of work. You now have a loop around the crochet hook on the RS of work.

NOTE: For a complete discussion of crochet techniques, see page 158 in the "Special Techniques" section.

*Chain 3 sts, push hook back into original stitch and sl st (bring the first loop over the last chain loop without wrapping yarn around hook). Single crochet 2 sts, sl st and rep from * around entire neck opening. When you are back at your starting place cut the yarn, fasten off, and weave in ends.

Work crochet picot trim around the armhole openings as for neckline, beg and ending at the underarm.

Finishing

Weave in all loose ends. Block dress.

Lass Hat

This hat is made from the bottom up. The seed stitch hatband is worked first, back and forth in rows. After it is complete, stitches at both ends of the band are bound off to form the ties. The remaining stitches are joined in the round and the remainder of the hat is worked in stockinette stitch.

SIZES
6–12 months (1–2 years, 2–4 years, 4–6 years, 6–8 years)

FINISHED MEASUREMENTS
Head circumference: 15 (17, 19, 20, 22)" [38 (43, 48, 51, 56)cm]

MATERIALS
Tahki/Stacy Charles *Cotton Classic* (100% mercerized cotton; 108 yd. [100m] per 50g skein): #3002 Black, 1 (1, 2, 2, 2) skeins
US 6 (4mm) 12" circular needle (for smallest size only)
US 6 (4mm) 16" circular needle (for all other sizes)
US 6 (4mm) double-pointed needles
US 4 (3.5mm) 16" circular needle
Stitch marker
Tapestry needle
Sewing needle
Sewing thread to match yarn
Row counter

GAUGE
18 sts and 24 rows = 4" (10cm) in St st on US 6 (4mm) needle, or size needed to obtain gauge

STITCH PATTERNS
Stockinette stitch worked in the round—Knit all stitches every round.
Seed stitch worked flat—On first row, *k1, p1; rep from * to end. On subsequent rows, purl the knits and knit the purls.
K2tog (see page 149)

Instructions

Hatband
With US 4 needle, CO 86 (94, 102, 110, 118) sts.
Rows 1, 3, and 5 (RS): *K1, p1; rep from * to end.
Rows 2, 4, and 6: *P1, k1; rep from * to end.

Row 7: BO 10 sts in patt, continue in patt to end of row—76 (84, 92, 100, 108) sts.
Row 8: Rep Row 7—66 (74, 82, 90, 98) sts.

Join for Hat Body
To knit the remainder of the hat, you will need to join the rem hatband stitches in the round.
Place marker, CO 2 sts, and join in the round—68 (76, 84, 92, 100) sts.
The remainder of the hat is worked in St st in the round.

Hat Body
Switch to US 6 needle (12" for smallest size and 16" for all other sizes) and knit in the round until hat measures 6 (6½, 7, 7½, 8)" [15 (17, 18, 19, 20)cm] from CO edge.

Crown Shaping
Rnd 1: *K15 (17, 19, 21, 23), k2tog; rep from * to end—64 (72, 80, 88, 96) sts.
Rnd 2: *K2, k2tog; rep from * to end—48 (54, 60, 66, 72) sts.
Rnd 3: Knit.
Rnd 4: *K1, k2tog; rep from * to end—32 (36, 40, 44, 48) sts.
Rnd 5: Knit.

Rnd 6: *K2tog; rep from * to end—16 (18, 20, 22, 24) sts.
Rnd 7: Rep Rnd 6—8 (9, 10, 11, 12) sts.
Rnd 8: *K2tog; rep from *; end k0 (1, 0, 1, 0)—4 (5, 5, 6, 6) sts.

Cut yarn, leaving a long tail. Thread a tapestry needle with the tail and run the needle through the rem stitches. Pull the tail taut to gather the hat top and then push the needle to the inside of the hat. Secure with a small back stitch, and weave in end.

Finishing

Weave in any rem ends. Block hat. Tie the hatband ends together. Secure hatband tie in place by sewing the ends to the hat with needle and thread (optional).

Mermaid

n shore or at sea, this cute outfit is sure to make a splash. Your little mermaid will love this top, skirt, and mermaid's purse. Made in breathable, cotton yarn, this set is ideal for summer days. She will be ready for fun in the sun in this adorable ensemble.

Sun Top

Girls of all ages will love this fun little top. Its silhouette and chevron shaping really capture the look of what a modern mermaid might wear. It is embellished, in true mermaid style, with beads and a few treasures from the sea.

Fishtail Skirt

The scalloped hem and paillette scales of this flouncy skirt mimic the fishy tail of a mermaid. Comfortable and fun to wear, this twirly skirt is bound to be a summer favorite.

Purse

This beach bag is the perfect size for toting a snack, towel, and change of clothes. With its sturdy base and fishnet sides, it is just what every bathing beauty needs for a day at the pool or a trip to the shore.

Sun Top

This design could not be simpler. It is essentially a stockinette tube worked from the top down. Paired increases and decreases create the chevron pattern and the neckline and hem shaping. Two lengths of I-cord form the straps. The top is embellished in mermaid style with a collection of seashells and beads sewn to the center front and hem of the garment.

SIZES
2 years (4 years, 6 years)

FINISHED MEASUREMENTS
Chest: 21 (23, 26)" [53 (58, 66)cm]

Sample size 4 years

MATERIALS
Tahki/Stacy Charles *Cotton Classic* (100% mercerized cotton; 108 yd. [100m] per 50g skein): #3807 Dark Turquoise (color A), 2 (2, 3) skeins; #3760 Bright Light Green (color B), 1 (1, 1) skein
US 5 (3.75mm) 16" circular needle (for sizes 2 and 4 only)
US 5 (3.75mm) 24" circular needle (for size 6 only)
US 3 (3.25mm) 16" circular needle
US 3 (3.25mm) double-pointed needles
Stitch markers
Row counter
Tapestry needle
Sewing needle
Sewing thread to match yarn
20–25 assorted shell beads and/or shell paillettes
1 yd. (1m) beading cord to match yarn

GAUGE
20 sts and 26 rows = 4" (10cm) in St st on US 5 (3.75mm) needle, or size needed to obtain gauge

STITCH PATTERNS
Stockinette stitch worked in the round—Knit all stitches every round.
Garter stitch worked in the round—Knit a round, purl a round.
K2tog (page 149)
K2tog tbl (page 150)
Ssk (page 150)
M1L (page 149)
M1R (page 149)

SPECIAL TECHNIQUES
I-cord (page 155)

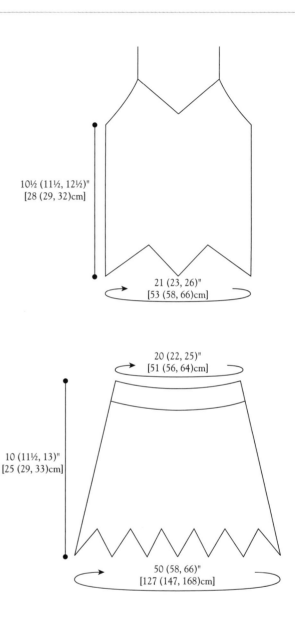

10½ (11½, 12½)" [28 (29, 32)cm]

21 (23, 26)" [53 (58, 66)cm]

20 (22, 25)" [51 (56, 64)cm]

10 (11½, 13)" [25 (29, 33)cm]

50 (58, 66)" [127 (147, 168)cm]

Instructions
Neckline Edging

With color B and US 3 circular needle, CO 128 (144, 160) sts, pm and join in the round. You will be placing 11 additional markers on the first round of the body. To avoid confusion, use markers that contrast with your original marker.

Rnds 1, 3, and 5: Purl.
Rnds 2 and 4: Knit.
Cut yarn.

Body

Switch to US 5 needle (16" for sizes 2 and 4 and 24" for size 6) and join color A.
Rnd 1: Beg at underarm, *k1, pm, k15 (17, 19), pm, k16 (18, 20), pm, k1 (center of V-neckline, front and back), pm, k16 (18, 20), pm, k15 (17, 19), pm (underarm); rep from *.
Rnd 2: *K1, sm, M1L, k13 (15, 17), k2tog tbl, sm, k2tog, k14 (16, 18), M1R, sm, k1 (center st), sm, M1L, k14 (16, 18), k2tog tbl, sm, k2tog, k13 (15, 17), M1R, sm; rep from *.
Rnd 3: *K1, sm, k15 (17, 19), sm, k16 (18, 20), sm, k1, sm, k16 (18, 20), sm, k15 (17, 19), sm; rep from *.

Rep Rnds 2 and 3 until top measures 10 (11, 12)" [25 (28, 30)cm] from CO edge, ending with Rnd 3. Cut yarn A.

Bottom Edging

Change to US 3 circular needle and color B.
Rnd 1: *K1, sm, M1L, k13 (15, 17), k2tog tbl, sm, k2tog, k14 (16, 18), M1R, sm, k1, sm, M1L, k14 (16, 18), k2tog tbl, sm, k2tog, k13 (15, 17), M1R, sm; rep from *.
Rnd 2: Purl.
Rnds 3–6: Rep Rnds 1 and 2.
BO all sts kwise. Cut yarn.

Shoulder Straps

With US 3 dpns and color B, CO 5 sts. Knit I-cord for 7 (8, 9)" [18 (20, 23)cm]. BO stitches. Cut yarn. Rep for second strap.

Attach Straps

NOTE: There are 31 (35, 39) underarm sts on each side (left and right) and 33 (37, 41) center sts on both the front and back. The straps are positioned on the points that separate these two sections.

Arrange work so that the armholes are to the sides and the V-neck shaping is in the center. With WS facing, pin the straps on the points of the CO edge of the sun top front or back. Sew in place.

Turn the sun top over and with WS facing, pin straps to the corresponding points on the other side of the piece. Sew in place.

Finishing

Weave in all ends. Block top.

Embellishments

With needle and thread sew one shell bead and one shell paillette to the points of the lower edge.

Thread an assortment of beads and paillettes, one at a time, onto two to three strands of 4–6" (10–15cm) beading cord. Tie a knot in the cord after every new addition. You can use the photo as a guide, but there is really no right and wrong way to arrange the beads and shells. It is a matter of personal preference. This is your chance to play. Pick an assortment of beads and arrange them in any way that is pleasing to you. No matter how you do it, it will be a fun and whimsical addition to the top.

NOTE: To safeguard the knots in your beading cord, paint a drop of clear nail polish or superglue onto the knot. Let dry completely before sewing cord to sweater.

Sew the strands of beading cord to the center of the V-neck edging. The fronts and the backs are identical so it doesn't matter which side you choose. With needle and thread, sew additional beads onto the center front.

Fishtail Skirt

This skirt is worked in the round from the top down. The elastic casing is worked in stockinette stitch and followed by the wave pattern of the skirt. Increases are worked in pattern as you make your way down to the hem of the skirt.

SIZES

2 years (4 years, 6 years)

FINISHED MEASUREMENTS

Waist: 20 (22, 25)" [51 (56, 64)cm]
Length: 10 (11¹/₂, 13)" [26 (29, 33)cm]

Sample size 4

MATERIALS

Tahki/Stacy Charles *Cotton Classic* (100% mercerized cotton; 108 yd. [100m] per 50g skein): #3760 Bright Light Green (color A), 1 (1, 1) skein; #3805 Turquoise (color B), 1 skein; #3783 Bright Teal (color C), 1 (1, 1) skein; #3807 Dark Turquoise (color D), 1 (1, 1) skein
US 5 (3.75mm) 24" circular needle
US 5 (3.75mm) 16" circular needle
US 4 (3.5mm) 24" circular needle
US 4 (3.5mm) 16" circular needle
Stitch markers
Stitch holder
Row counter
Tapestry needle
Sewing needle
Sewing thread to match yarn
20 shell paillettes or beads, ¹/₂" size
30 shell paillettes or beads, ¹/₄" size
20 (22, 25)" [51 (56, 64)cm] of 1" (3cm) elastic
Large safety pin

GAUGE

20 sts and 26 rows = 4" (10cm) in St st on US 5 (3.75mm) needle, or size needed to obtain gauge

STITCH PATTERNS

Stockinette stitch worked in the round—Knit all stitches every round.
Garter stitch worked in the round—Knit a round, purl a round.
K2tog (page 149)
K2tog tbl (page 150)
M1L (page 149)
M1R (page 149)

Instructions

Waistband

With 16" US 4 and color A, CO 110 (130, 150) sts, pm and join in the round, taking care not to twist stitches.
Knit 7 rnds for waistband facing.
Purl 1 rnd for waistband turning ridge.
Knit 7 rnds for waistband. Cut yarn A.

Skirt Body

This skirt is worked in a striped wave stitch pattern. As you work the skirt, you will be working the stripe pattern and the wave stitch pattern at the same time. The shaping of the skirt is worked along the way, with increase rounds spaced throughout the skirt body. The instructions for the Stripe Pattern, the Wave Stitch, and the Increase Rounds are listed below, followed by the instructions for how to begin and complete the Skirt Body.

Stripe Pattern
Knit 8 rounds color B.
Knit 8 rounds color C.
Knit 8 rounds color D.

Wave Stitch
Rnd 1: Knit.
Rnd 2: *K2tog, k3 (4, 5), M1R, pm, k1, pm, M1L, k3 (4, 5), k2tog tbl, pm; rep from * to end.
Rep Rnds 1 and 2 for Wave patt, slipping markers instead of placing them and simultaneously working stripe patt.

Increase Round
*Knit to first marker, M1R, sm, k1, sm, M1L, k to next marker, sm; rep from * to end of round—20 sts increased.

NOTE: All Increase Rnds are worked on and in place of Rnd 2 of the Wave Stitch patt.

Use 16" US 5 needle and color B to begin the skirt body. Switch to the 24" US 5 needle as your stitch count increases and the stitches become crowded on the 16" needle.

Begin working stripe patt and wave patt simultaneously, twisting yarns together at the beg of every other round and carrying the colors not in use up the inside of the skirt.

When beginning a new stripe, bring the new color under the last color used.

At the same time, shape skirt by working the Inc Rnd on the eighth round of the first stripe. After the first increase you will work the Inc Rnd every sixth round four times to 210 (230, 250) sts. End by working the Inc Rnd every eighth round 2 (3, 4) times—250 (290, 330) sts. Cut yarns B, C, and D, leaving tails long enough to weave in later.

Hem

Change to 24" US 4 needle and color A.
Work 6 rounds of garter stitch as follows.
Rnds 1, 3, and 5: *K2tog, k to marker, M1R, sm, k1, sm, M1L, k to 2 sts before next marker, k2tog tbl, sm; rep from * to end.
Rnds 2, 4, and 6: Purl.
BO all sts kwise, cut yarn and fasten off.

Finishing

Weave in any ends. Block skirt.

Sew Waistband

Cut 20 (22, 25)" [51 (56, 64)cm] length elastic. Turn the skirt inside out and fold facing to the WS of skirt at the turning ridge (purl round). Pin in place. Thread tapestry needle with color A and sew the facing to the waistband. When you have made your way to within 2" (5cm) from where you started, stop sewing, but do not cut yarn. Put a safety pin through the end of the elastic and thread it through the casing. Sew the two ends of the elastic together. Return to the casing edge and finish sewing it in place.

Embellishments

With a needle and thread, sew paillettes to skirt using photo as a guide. This is just one way to bead the skirt. Embellish however you wish ... shells and beads all over or just on the hem, either way is cute.

Purse

This bag is worked in the round from the bottom up. The base is worked in garter stitch, and the sides are worked in a stockinette wave pattern ending with the netting border. The handles are knitted onto the upper edge of the bag, in garter stitch. The bag is decorated with beads and seashells sewn to the net section of the bag.

FINISHED MEASUREMENTS
The following are flat measurements, taken with the bag empty. Because of the stretchy nature of the stitches, this bag will easily accommodate the basic needs of any bathing beauty.

Base diameter: 10" (25cm)
Circumference: 25" (64cm)
Height from base to upper edge: 10½" (27cm)

MATERIALS
Tahki/Stacy Charles *Cotton Classic* (100% mercerized cotton; 108 yd. [100m] per 50g skein): #3870 Dark Bright Blue (color A), 2 skeins; #3760 Bright Light Green (color B), 1 skein; #3786 Dark Teal (color C), 1 skein; #3783 Bright Teal (color D), 1 skein; #3807 Dark Turquoise (color E), 1 skein; #3805 Turquoise (color F), 1 skein
US 5 (3.75mm) 24" circular needle
US 4 (3.5mm) 16" circular needle
US 4 (3.5mm) double-pointed needles
Stitch markers of several contrasting colors
Stitch holder
Row counter
Tapestry needle
Sewing needle and thread
15–20 assorted shell beads, seashells, or paillettes

GAUGE
20 sts and 26 rows = 4" (10cm) in St st on US 5 (3.75mm) needle, or size needed to obtain gauge

STITCH PATTERNS
Stockinette stitch worked in the round—Knit all stitches every round.
Garter stitch worked flat—Knit all stitches every row.
Garter stitch worked in the round—Knit a round, purl a round.
K2tog (page 149)
P2tog (page 150)
M1 (page 149)
Yo (page 148)

SPECIAL TECHNIQUES
Three-needle bind-off (page 151)

Instructions

Base

With color A and US 4 dpns, CO 6 sts. Divide evenly onto 4 needles. Knit across, placing a marker after each of the first 5 sts. Place a contrasting marker after the sixth stitch to mark the beginning of the round (6 markers placed). Join work in the round, taking care not to twist stitches.

Rnd 1: Purl.
Rnd 2: *K1, M1, sm; rep from * to end—12 sts.

Repeat Rnds 1 and 2, switching to US 4 circular needle when dpns become too crowded. Continue until you have 23 sts in between the markers, ending with a purl round—138 sts. Cut yarn.

Garter Ridge

The Garter Ridge is worked between each section of the bag. It is always worked the same way and always with color B.

Switch to US 5 needle and join color B.
Work 6 rounds of garter stitch (knit a round, purl a round). Keep the markers in place, slipping them as you go. End with a purl round. Cut color B.

Bag Body

You will place twelve new markers on the first round of this patt section. Do not discard the markers that are already in place. Both sets of markers will be used in the patt. The new set of markers indicate where to work the yarn overs in the patt and the existing markers indicate the end of each patt repeat. To avoid confusion, use markers that contrast with the ones already in place, making sure that the marker indicating the beg of the round is different from all the rest.

Wave Pattern
Switch to color C.
Rnd 1 and all odd rnds: *K11, pm, k1, pm, k11, sm from previous rounds; rep from * around. On rem odd rnds, do not place new markers; slip all markers from previous rounds.

Rnd 2 and all even rnds: *K2tog, k9, yo, sm, k1, sm, yo, k9, k2tog, sm; rep from * around.

Work the rem rounds of this section in the Wave Pattern as established in Rnds 1 and 2, slipping markers as you go, and working the Stripe Sequence listed below.

Stripe Sequence
Rnds 3 and 4: Color D.
Rnds 5 and 6: Color E.
Rnds 7 and 8: Color F.
Rnds 9 and 10: Color E.
Rnds 11 and 12: Color D.
Rnds 13 and 14: Color C.
Rnds 15 and 16: Color A.
Rnds 17 and 18: Color C.
Rnds 19 and 20: Color D.
Rnds 21 and 22: Color E.
Rnds 23 and 24: Color F.
Rnds 25 and 26: Color E.
Rnds 27 and 28: Color D.
Rnds 29 and 30: Color C.
Cut color C.

Garter Ridge

Switch to color B and work Garter Ridge.
Cut color B.

Netting

Join color E.
Rnd 1: *K2tog, yo; rep from * to end.
Rnd 2: *P2tog, yo; rep from * to end.

Rep Rnds 1 and 2 until netting section measures 3" (8cm), measured flat without stretching, ending with Rnd 2.
Next rnd: Still using color E, knit.
Cut color E.

Garter Ridge

Switch to color B and work Garter Ridge.
Cut color B.

Bag Edging and Handles

Switch to color A.

Rnd 1: Knit.

Rnd 2: BO 10 sts, p10, BO 29 sts, p10, BO 20 sts, p10, BO 29 sts, p10, BO rem stitches.

Four groups of 5 sts rem on the needle, each group has 10 sts—40 sts total. These stitches are the base row of each of the handles. The handles are worked individually in garter stitch rows, beg at the edge of the bag. Once all of the handles are complete, they will be seamed together with a three-needle bind-off.

*With RS facing and a US 4 dpn, join color A and knit across the first group of 10 sts on the 24" needle. Work on this group of stitches, using the US 4 dpns and knitting every row, until the handle is 5½" (14cm) long, ending with a WS row. Leave these stitches on the dpn and move to the next set of handle stitches on the 24" needle.

Rep from * for rem three straps, knitting them in the order that they were worked in the round.

When you have made all four straps, turn the bag inside out. Pair the needle holding the first strap together with the needle holding the second strap. Hold the needles together so that they are parallel to one other and work a three-needle bind-off. Cut yarn and fasten off. Rep three-needle bind-off with the third and fourth straps.

Finishing

Weave in any ends. Block bag if desired.

Embellishments

With a needle and thread, sew shells, paillettes, and/or beads to the netted section of the bag.

Princess

now White, Sleeping Beauty, the Princess and the Pea ... so many princesses ....

A book of fairy tale knits would hardly be complete without something for the aspiring princess. This sparkly sweater is made in classic princess fashion with puff sleeves and lacey details. Pretty but not fussy, it is a modern take on the traditional dress. Pair it with a skirt, jeans, or even a tutu, for your own happily ever after.

Sweater

This sweater is worked in the round from the bottom up. At the underarms, stitches are divided for the front and back, and the remainder of the sweater bodice is worked back and forth in rows. A three-needle bind-off joins the shoulder seams. Stitches are picked up along the armhole openings for the sleeves, and they are knit in the round from the armhole edge to the cuff. A combination of increases, short rows, and decreases shape the puff sleeves. The mitered neckline is worked in the round in garter stitch.

SIZES

2 years (4 years, 5 years, 6 years)

FINISHED MEASUREMENTS

Chest: 22 (24, 26, 27)" [56 (61, 66, 69)cm]
Length from shoulder to hem: 13¹/₂ (14¹/₂, 15¹/₂, 16¹/₂)" [34 (37, 39, 42)cm]

Sample size 2 years

MATERIALS

Patons *Brilliant* (69% acrylic, 19% nylon, 12% polyester; 166 yd. [151m]
    per 50g skein): #3314 Lilac Luster, 4 (5, 5, 6) skeins
US 5 (3.75mm) 16" circular needle
US 5 (3.75mm) 24" circular needle
US 5 (3.75mm) double-pointed needles
US 3 (3.25mm) 16" circular needle
US 3 (3.25mm) 24" circular needle
US 3 (3.25mm) double-pointed needles

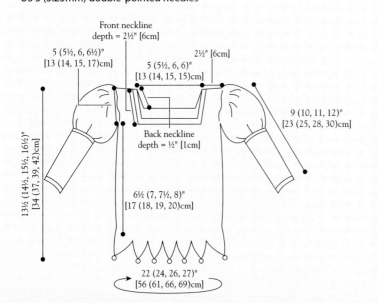

Front neckline
depth = 2½" [6cm]

5 (5½, 6, 6½)"
[13 (14, 15, 17)cm]

2½" [6cm]

5 (5½, 6, 6)"
[13 (14, 15, 15)cm]

9 (10, 11, 12)"
[23 (25, 28, 30)cm]

Back neckline
depth = ½" [1cm]

13½ (14½, 15½, 16½)"
[34 (37, 39, 42)cm]

6½ (7, 7½, 8)"
[17 (18, 19, 20)cm]

22 (24, 26, 27)"
[56 (61, 66, 69)cm]

Row counter
Stitch markers
Stitch holders
Tapestry needle
2 small safety pins

GAUGE

26 sts and 34 rows = 4" (10cm) in St st on US 5 needles, or size
    needed to obtain gauge

STITCH PATTERNS

Stockinette stitch worked in the round—Knit all stitches
    every round.
Stockinette stitch worked flat—Knit on RS rows, purl on WS
    rows.
MB (make bobble)—K1, p1, k1 in the next st, turn, *k1, p1, k1,
    turn; rep from * 2 times, k1, p1, k1, pass 2nd and 3rd sts over
    1st st.
K2tog (page 149)
Skpo (page 151)
Sk2po (page 151)
Ssk (page 150)
W&t (page 154)
Yo (page 148)

SPECIAL TECHNIQUES

Three-needle bind-off (page 151)
Short rows (page 154)

Instructions

Lace Border

With 24" US 5 needle, CO 180 (200, 210, 220) sts, pm after every tenth stitch and place a contrasting marker after the last stitch.

Join in the round and work Preparatory Rnd, slipping markers as you come to them.

Preparatory Rnd: *P4, MB, p5; rep from * across.
Rnd 1: *Yo, k3, sk2po, k3, yo, k1; rep from * across.
Rnd 2: Knit.
Rnd 3: *K1, yo, k2, sk2po, k2, yo, k1, p1; rep from * across.
Rnds 4 and 6: *K9, p1; rep from * across.
Rnd 5: *K2, yo, k1, sk2po, k1, yo, k2, p1; rep from * across.
Rnd 7: *K3, yo, sk2po, yo, k3, p1; rep from * across.
Rnd 8: Knit.

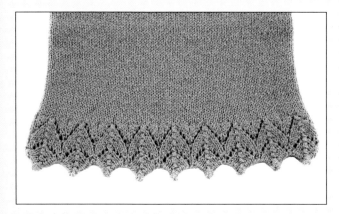

Rnds 9–16: Rep Rnds 1–8.
Rnd 17: *K2, ssk, k1, k2tog, k3, discard marker; rep from * to end leaving the contrasting marker in place—144 (160, 168, 176) sts.

Switch to the 16" US 5 needle for smallest size sweater only.

Sweater Body

Knit 72 (80, 84, 88) sts, pm, knit to end of round. Continue to knit in St st until the piece measures 6½ (7, 7½, 8)" [17 (18, 19, 20)cm] from last row of lace border (Row 17).

Divide for Front and Back

From this point on the sweater will be worked back and forth in St st rows. You will work the back of the sweater first. The stitches for the sweater front will be held in reserve for later.

K1, ssk, k66 (74, 78, 82), k2tog, k1—70 (78, 82, 86) sts. Turn and purl back across these same stitches. These are the stitches that will form the sweater back. Put rem 72 (80, 84, 88) sts for the sweater front on a spare needle or holder for later.

Back Armhole Shaping

In the following rows, you will continue the armhole shaping that you began when you divided the stitches for the front and back of the sweater.

Row 1 (RS): K1, ssk, k to last 3 sts, k2tog, k1—68 (76, 80, 84) sts.

Row 2 (WS): Purl.
Rep last two rows 3 (4, 4, 4) times—62 (68, 72, 76) sts.

Place a safety pin on the right and left edge, of the sweater to mark the last row of the armhole shaping.

Continue to work remainder of sweater back without shaping until piece measures 4 (4½, 5, 5½)" [10 (11, 13, 14)cm] from beg of armhole, ending with a WS row.

Back Neck and Shoulder Shaping

The shoulders are worked one at a time, beg with the right shoulder.

Right Shoulder

With RS facing, k12 (13, 14, 15), turn. These are the right shoulder stitches.

Place rem 50 (55, 58, 61) sts for the center neck and left shoulder on a holder or spare needle to be worked later.

Continue working in St st on the 12 (13, 14, 15) sts for right shoulder only, until the armhole edge measures 5 (5½, 6, 6½)" [13 (14, 15, 17)cm], ending with a WS row. Cut yarn.

Place stitches for right shoulder on a holder.

Left Shoulder

With RS facing, join yarn at the neck edge of the right shoulder, knit across the stitches on reserve for the back of the neck and the left shoulder. At the end of the row, turn and purl across 12 (13, 14, 15) sts for the left shoulder. Put center 38 (42, 44, 46) sts on a holder for back of neck.

Work left shoulder in St st as for right shoulder, ending with a WS row. Place left shoulder stitches on a holder for later.

Sweater Front

With RS facing and beginning at the left armhole edge, join yarn and work armhole shaping as for sweater back until 62 (68, 72, 76) sts rem.

Continue to work in St st without further shaping until the armhole measures 2 (2½, 3, 3½)" [5 (6, 8, 9)cm], ending with a WS row. Begin neck shaping.

Front Neck and Shoulder Shaping

Work front neck shaping as for back, putting center sts on a holder, working each shoulder one at a time, and continuing to work in St st until the neck edge is 3" (8cm) long and the front and back armhole lengths are equal. End with a WS row. Cut yarn.

Shoulder Seams

Turn the sweater inside out so that the RS of the sweater are together. Place each set of shoulder stitches onto a separate US 5 dpn. With WS facing and beg at the right armhole edge, join yarn and work a three-needle bind-off to join the front and back right shoulder stitches together. Cut yarn. Leave the stitches for the center of the neck on the holders.

Rep for left shoulder seam, working from the left armhole to the neck edge.

Neckband

Slide the front and back center stitches onto two separate US 3 dpns.

With 16" US 3 needle, RS of sweater back facing, and beg at the corner where the center back and the left neck edge meet, pick up 26 sts evenly along the left neck edge ending at the corner where the left neck edge and the center front meet, pm, k across 40 (42, 44, 46) sts for the center front, pm, pick up 26 sts evenly along right neck edge, ending at the corner where the right neck edge and the center back meet, pm, k across 40 (42, 44, 46) sts for center back neck, place a contrasting marker—132 (136, 140, 144) sts.

Rnd 1: Join work in the round and purl.
Rnd 2: K2tog, *k to 2 sts before marker, skpo, sm, k2tog; rep from * around, end skpo—124 (128, 132, 136) sts.
Rnd 3: Purl.
Rnds 4 and 5: Rep Rows 2 and 3—116 (120, 124, 128) sts.
Rnd 6: BO all stitches kwise, working dec at the corners as for Rnd 2 at the same time.

Sleeves

With RS facing and beg at the base of the armhole edge use US 3 dpns to pick up 7 (7, 8, 8) sts between the base of

the armhole and the last dec worked for the armhole shaping. Remove the safety pin and place a marker on the needle (this marker will be referred to as marker A). Pick up 52 (56, 60, 64) sts between this point and the safety pin marking the armhole shaping on the opposite side of the sleeve, remove safety pin and place a second marker on the needle (marker B). End by picking up 7 (7, 8, 8) sts between marker B and the base of the armhole (where you started). Place a contrasting marker to indicate the end of the round—66 (70, 76, 80) sts.

Begin Puff Sleeve

To form the gathers at the top of the puff sleeves, you will work an increase in each stitch between markers A and B. Since the stitch count between these two markers will be doubled, you may want to use a 16" needle until you gather the sleeve for the sleeve binding.

Join work in the round. K to marker A, sm, *k1, kfb; rep from * to marker B, sm, k to end of round (contrasting marker)—92 (98, 106, 112) total sts in round.

Switch to 16" US 5 or US 5 dpns.

Short Rows

The upper portion of the sleeve is shaped with short rows. This builds up the top of the sleeve while avoiding extra bulk at the underarm.

NOTE: For a complete discussion of short rows, see page 154 in the "Special Techniques" section.

Set-up row: K to marker A, sm, k to marker B, sm, k1, w&t next stitch, p back to marker A, sm, p1, w&t next st.
Row 1: K to marker B, sm, k2, w&t next stitch, p back to marker A, sm, p2, w&t next stitch.
Row 2: K to marker B, sm, k3, w&t next stitch, p back to marker A, sm, p3, w&t next stitch.
Row 3: K to marker B, sm, k4, w&t next stitch, p back to marker A, sm, p4, w&t next stitch.
Row 4: K to marker B, sm, k5, w&t next stitch, p back to marker A, sm, p5, w&t next stitch.
This is the last short row for sizes 2 and 4, skip Row 5 and go on to "End Short Rows."

Row 5 (for sizes 5 and 6 only): K to marker
B, sm, k6, w&t next stitch, p back to marker
A, sm, p6, w&t next stitch.

End Short Rows

Beg with RS of work facing and the stitch that
you just wrapped on the RH needle, knit to
the end of the round (back to the contrasting
marker) without wrapping and turning. From
here on, the sleeve will be knit in St st in the
round without short-rowing.

Continue Puff Sleeve

Knit 3 rounds plain.
Dec Rnd: K1, ssk, k to last 3 sts, k2tog,
k1—90 (96, 104, 110) sts.
Rep last four rounds 4 times—82 (88, 96, 102).
Continue tin St st for 1½ (2, 2, 2½)" [4 (5, 5,
6)cm].

Gather Puff Sleeve

Switch to US 5 dpns.
K2tog around—41 (44, 48, 51) sts.

Puff Sleeve Binding

Rnd 1: Purl.
Rnd 2: Knit.
Rnds 3–8: Rep Rnds 1 and 2.

Work Lower Sleeve

Knit St st until sleeve measures 8½ (9½, 10½,
11½)" [22 (24, 27, 29)cm] from underarm.

Sleeve Cuff

Switch to US 4 dpns.
Rnd 1: Purl.
Rnd 2: Knit.
Rnds 3–6: Rep Rnds 1 and 2.
Rnd 7: Purl.
Rnd 8: BO kwise. Cut yarn.

Repeat for second sleeve.

Finishing

Weave in all ends. Block sweater.

The Castle

This set is just what every young knight needs to decorate his castle in style. Knit in colorful worsted weight wool and felted to a dense fabric, this banner and pair of pillows are sure to please all the members of your court.

Banner/Valance

Hang this attractive banner on a wall or use it as a valance over a window or door to make your child feel truly regal. The lion and shield on this wall covering are inspired by designs found in medieval armor and tapestries. Your young prince will feel like the king of the castle with this imperial design decorating his bedroom walls.

Royal Colors Pillow

Plump and sturdy, this pillow is perfect for naptime, playtime or an afternoon with a good book. Knit it in the royal purple, crimson, and gold as shown, or use the colors of your own crest to create a room accessory that is sure to please any young knight.

Lion Pillow

The color and design of this striking cushion mirror that of the banner. Just the right size for playtime and bedtime, this comfy pillow is a welcome addition to knightly quarters. This handsome design will transform any child's ordinary room into a royal bedchamber.

Banner/Valance

This pattern is worked from the bottom up, on large needles with two strands of yarn held together throughout. The panels forming the crenellated border are worked individually and are joined together to form the base of the banner. The colorwork is knitted in intarsia, but could also be worked in duplicate stitch. Felting finishes the banner, making the fabric smooth and seemingly stitchless.

FINISHED MEASUREMENTS
Before Felting
38" × 25½" (97cm × 65cm)

After Felting
31" × 18" (79cm × 46cm)

MATERIALS
Patons *Classic Merino Wool* (100% pure wool; 223 yd. [204m] per 100 g skein): #00212 Royal Purple (color A), 1 skein; #00207 Rich Red (color B), 5 skeins; #00204 Old Gold (color C), 1 skein
US 11 (8mm) 32" circular needle
Row counter
Stitch markers
Stitch holders
Row counter
Tapestry needle
Bobbins (optional)
10 clip-on or sew-on curtain rings
Dowel or curtain rod (optional)
Sewing needle and thread (optional)

GAUGE
11 sts and 14 rows = 4" (10cm) in St st with double-stranded yarn using US 11 (8mm) needles, or size needed to obtain gauge

NOTE: If you decide to use different yarn to make this project, look for comparable wool yarn that by itself has a gauge of 18–20 sts per 4" (10cm) in St st on US 7–8 (4.5–5mm) needles.

STITCH PATTERNS
Stockinette stitch worked flat—Knit on RS rows; purl on WS rows.
Garter stitch worked flat—Knit all stitches every row.

SPECIAL TECHNIQUES
Intarsia (page 157)
Felting (page 160)

Instructions
NOTE: This pattern is worked with two strands of yarn held together throughout.

Crenellated Border
Three panels are worked individually and are joined together, with additional stitches worked in between each panel, to form the body of the banner. The colorwork on each panel is worked using intarsia.

NOTE: Because you do not carry the yarn across the back of the work when changing colors in intarsia, you will need to twist the yarns together to prevent an unwanted hole from forming where the color change occurs. To do this on RS rows, pick up the new yarn from underneath the yarn just used. On WS rows, drop the yarn just used and bring the new yarn up and to the right of the yarn just used to twist the yarns.

In preparation for the colorwork in this pattern, wind several bobbins (double stranded) of colors A, B, and C. You will need a bobbin of color A for each side of each panel, separate balls of yarn in color B for the center of each panel and several bobbins in color C for the shield.

Using a double strand of color A, CO 22 sts.
Rows 1–3: Knit.
Row 4 (RS): K3 color A, join a double strand of color B and k16, k3 color A.
Row 5 (WS): K3 color A, p16 color B, k3 color A.
Rows 6–13: Rep Rows 4 and 5.

Cut yarn and put stitches onto a holder or spare needle for later. Rep the above steps twice more for the other two panels. Keep the panel you worked last on the needle. Do not cut yarn.

Join the Panels
With RS facing, work across the first panel, maintaining color and stitch patt. Do not turn work. *Keep the needle holding the stitches you just worked in your right hand, and continuing with color A, use the backward loop method (see page 145) to CO 16 sts. Join second panel with RS facing, and work across it as for Row 4. Rep from * casting on additional stitches, joining and working the third panel as established above—98 sts. Turn work.

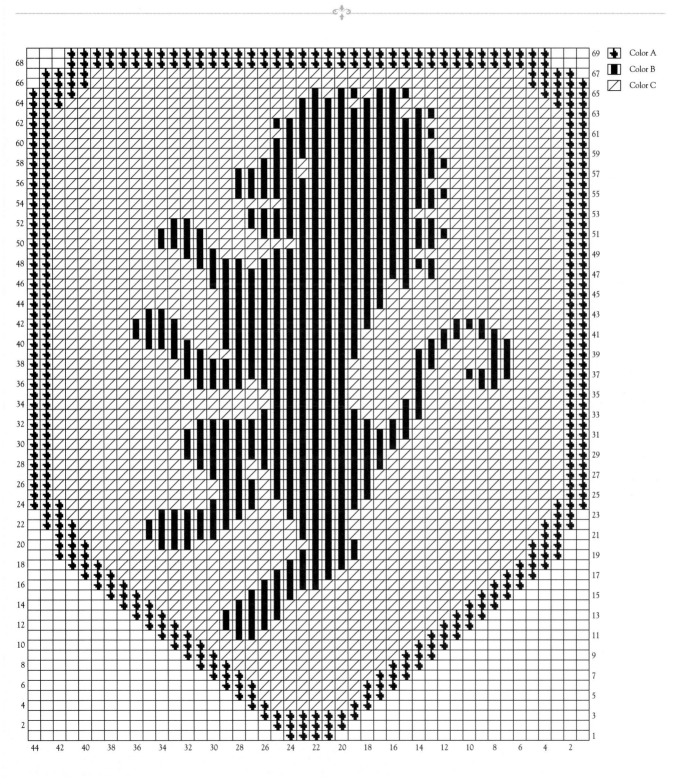

Color A
Color B
Color C

Banner Body

Work the next five rows as follows:

Rows 1 and 3 (WS): K3 color A, *p16 color B, k22 color A; rep from * once to rem 19 sts, p16 color B, k3 color A.

Rows 2 and 4 (RS): K3 color A, *k16 color B, k22 color A; rep from * once to rem 19 sts, k16 color B, k3 color A.

Row 5: K3 color A, p92 color B, k3 color A.

Work Chart

As you work across the next two rows, you will be establishing the patt for working the charted section of the banner. The chart is worked across the center 44 sts of the banner. There are 27 sts on each side of the charted motif. Markers to the left and right of this section isolate the charted area from the rest of the banner.

The chart for this pattern is worked in St st from the bottom up, from right to left on RS rows and from left to right on WS rows. The empty blocks in the chart are part of the background of the banner and should be worked in color B.

Begin the chart with a RS row. Always knit the odd rows of the chart and purl the even rows.

Next row and all odd rows of chart (RS): K3 color A, k24 color B, pm, k across chart from right to left, bottom to top (beg with Row 1), joining colors as needed, place a second marker, k24 color B, k3 color A.

Next row and all even rows of chart (WS): K3 color A, p24, sm, p across the next row of the chart from left to right (beg with Row 2), sm, p24 color B, k3 color A.

Continue working as established, knitting a garter stitch border in color A at the beg and end of every row, and working the chart and background in St st (with the chart centered on color B background) until all 69 rows of chart are complete, ending with a RS row.

NOTE: Download a full-size version of the banner/valance work chart at www.wiley.com/go/fairytaleknits.

Work Remainder of Banner

Next row (WS): K3 color A, p92 color B, k3 color A.
Next row (RS): K3 color A, k92 color B, k3 color A.

Rep last two rows once, then work one more WS row as established, for a total of five rows.

Upper Edging

Beg with a RS row, knit 5 rows color A.
BO kwise.

Finishing

Weave in all loose ends.

Felting and Blocking

Place the banner in a zippered pillowcase or mesh laundry bag and felt it as per instructions on page 160. Place the banner on a towel and pull it into the desired shape and measurements. Let the piece air dry, flipping it over as necessary.

Assembly

Attach curtain rings to the upper border of the banner.

Royal Colors Pillow

The color-block design of this pillow offers a manageable introduction to intarsia colorwork. This pattern is worked in one piece, starting with the button flap and continuing on to the pillow front and back. After the knitting is complete, two side seams bring the pillow together and then it's off to the washer for felting. The felting process leaves the surface of the fabric smooth, making it the perfect palette for embellishing with beads, buttons, pompoms, or embroidery.

FINISHED MEASUREMENTS
Before Felting
15" × 17½" (38cm × 44cm)
After Felting
14½" × 10½" (37cm × 27cm)

MATERIALS

Patons *Classic Merino Wool* (100% pure wool; 223 yd. [204m] per 100g skein): #00212 Royal Purple (color A), 1 skein; #00207 Rich Red (color B), 1 skein; #00204 Old Gold (color C), 1 skein
US 11 (8mm) 24" or 32" circular needle
Row counter
Bobbins (optional)
Tapestry needle
Wool fleece or Polyfil
1/2"–1" (1cm–3cm) decorative buttons—4
Beads (for optional embellishing)
Embroidery floss to match yarn (optional for embellishing)
Sewing needle
Sewing thread to match pillow

GAUGE

11 sts and 14 rows = 4" (10cm) in St st with double-stranded yarn using US 11 (8mm) needles, or size needed to obtain gauge

NOTE: If you decide to use different yarn to make this project, look for wool yarn that by itself has a gauge of 18–20 sts per 4" (10cm) in St st on US 7–8 (4.5–5mm) needles.

STITCH PATTERNS

Stockinette stitch worked flat—Knit on RS rows; purl on WS rows.
Garter stitch worked flat—Knit all stitches every row.

SPECIAL TECHNIQUES

Intarsia (page 157)
Felting (page 160)
Pompoms (page 155)

Instructions

NOTE: This pattern is worked with two strands of yarn held together throughout.

Button Flap

Using a double strand of color A, CO 46 sts.
Work in garter stitch for 14 rows, knitting all rows.

Turning Ridge (RS): Purl.
Next row (WS): Knit.

Pillow Front

NOTE: Because you do not carry the yarn across the back of the work when changing colors in intarsia, you will need to twist the yarns together to prevent a hole from forming where the color change occurs. To do this on RS rows, pick up the new yarn from underneath the yarn just used. On WS rows, drop the yarn just used and bring the new yarn up and to the right of the yarn just used to twist the yarns.

In preparation of the colorwork for this pattern, you will need to wind several bobbins. You will need two bobbins of color A, three bobbins of color B, and one of color C to get started.

Rows 1–6: Knit color A.
Row 7 (RS): K6 color A, join color B and k34, join color A and k6.
Row 8: K6 color A, p34 color B, k6 color A.
Row 9: K6 color A, k2 color B, k15 color A, k15 color C, k2 color B, k6 color A.
Row 10: K6 color A, p2 color B, p15 color C, p15 color A, p2 color B, k6 color A.
Rows 11–28: Rep Rows 9 and 10.
Row 29: K6 color A, k2 color B, k15 color C, k15 color A, k2 color B, k6 color A.
Row 30: K6 color A, p2 color B, p15 color A, p15 color C, p2 color B, k6 color A.
Rows 31–48: Rep Rows 29 and 30.

Row 49: K6 color A, k34 color B, k6 color A.
Row 50: K6 color A, p34 color B, k6 color A.
Cut colors B and C.
Rows 51–56: Knit color A.
Work turning ridge (RS): Purl color A.

Pillow Back

Knit all rows with color A until the length of the back matches the length of the pillow front, not including the button flap.
BO kwise.

Pompoms

Make 4 pompoms as per instructions in on page 155.

Finishing

Weave in all ends.
With WS together, fold the pillow into an envelope shape at the lower turning ridge and pin into place. To sew side seams, thread a tapestry needle with a length of color A. Starting at the lower turning ridge, insert needle into the bottom loop of the first selvedge stitch on the pillow front and then into the top loop of corresponding purl stitch on pillow back. Continue working back and forth up to the CO edge of the pillow. Leave the flap side of the pillow open. It will be sewn in place after felting.

Felting and Blocking

Felt and block the pillow as instructed in on page 160.

Assembly

Embellish the pillow back by sewing decorative buttons, evenly spaced, across flap. Stuff the pillow with wool fleece or Polyfil. Fold the flap down so that it covers the CO edge and pin into place. Sew flap to pillow back along side seams and across the CO edge. Sew pompoms to pillow corners. Embellish the front of the pillow as desired with additional buttons, beads, or embroidery.

Lion Pillow

This pattern is worked on large needles with two strands of yarn held together throughout. The pillow back, front, and button flap are knitted as one piece. Two side seams bring the piece together after the knitting is complete. The lion motif and borders are worked using intarsia. If intarsia is not your thing, the same effect can be achieved with duplicate stitch. The real magic of this project happens in the felting process, during which the individual stitches disappear.

FINISHED MEASUREMENTS

Before Felting
18¹/₂" × 24" (47cm × 61cm)

After Felting
15³/₄" × 14" (40cm × 36cm)

MATERIALS

Patons *Classic Merino Wool* (100% pure wool; 223 yd. [204m] per 100g skein): #00212 Royal Purple (color A), 1 skein; #00207 Rich Red (color B), 1 skein; #00204 Old Gold (color C), 1 skein
US 11 (8mm) 24" or 32" circular needle
Row counter
Bobbins (optional)
Tapestry needle
Wool fleece or Polyfil
¹/₂"–1" (1cm–3cm) decorative buttons—4
Sewing needle
Sewing thread to match pillow

GAUGE

11 sts and 14 rows = 4" (10cm) in St st with double-stranded yarn using US 11 (8mm) needles, or size needed to obtain gauge.

NOTE: If you decide to use different yarn to make this project, look for yarn that by itself has a gauge of 18–20 sts per 4" (10cm) in St st on US 7–8 (4.5–5mm) needles.

STITCH PATTERNS

Stockinette stitch worked flat—Knit on RS rows; purl on WS rows.
Garter stitch worked flat—Knit all stitches every row.

SPECIAL TECHNIQUES

Intarsia (page 157)
Felting (page 160)
Pompoms (page 155)
Duplicate stitch (page 157)

Instructions

NOTE: All yarn is double-stranded, two strands held as one, throughout this pattern.

Button Flap

Using a double-strand of color A, CO 50 sts.
Work in garter stitch for 14 rows, knitting all rows.

Work turning ridge (RS): Purl color A. See instructions for other pillow.
Turning Ridge (RS): Purl.
Next row (WS): Knit.

Pillow Front

Garter Stitch Border

Beg the front of the pillow by working a garter stitch border, knitting 6 rows of color A and ending with a WS row.

In preparation of the colorwork, you will need to wind several bobbins (double stranded)—one to two of color A, three to four of color B, and two of color C.

Work Chart

You will continue to work garter stitch in color A at the left and right edges of the pillow front, working the chart across the center 38 sts in St st. Work chart from right to left on all odd rows, knitting all stitches, and from left to right on all even rows, purling all stitches.

The chart for this pattern is worked from the bottom up, from right to left on the RS rows and from left to right on the WS rows.

NOTE: Because you do not carry the yarn across the back of the work when changing colors in intarsia, you will need to twist the yarns together to prevent a hole from forming where the color change occurs. To do this on RS rows, pick up the new yarn from underneath the yarn just used. On WS rows, drop the yarn just used and bring the new yarn up and to the right of the yarn just used to twist the yarns.

Row 1 (RS): K6 color A, join a double-strand of color B and k Row 1 of chart across next 38 sts, join color A and k6.
Row 2: K6 color A, p across Row 2 of chart, k6 color A.

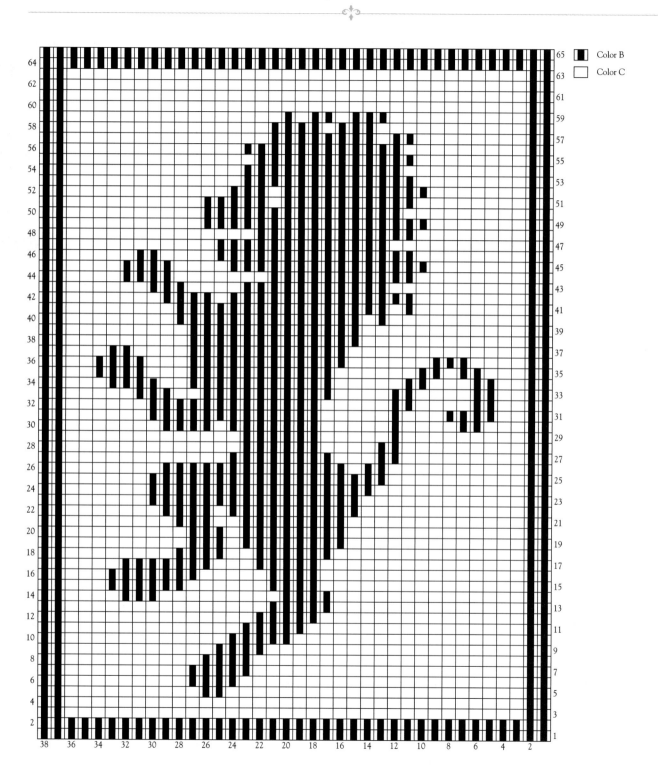

Rows 3–65: Continue working patt as established, using all three colors and centering the 38 sts of the chart between 6 sts of color A on each end, ending with a RS row. Cut colors B and C.

NOTE: Download a full-size version of the lion work chart at www.wiley.com/go/fairytaleknits.

Garter Stitch Border
Finish the front of the pillow with a garter stitch border, knitting 5 rows of color A and ending with a WS row.

Pillow Back

Knit all rows with color A until the length of the back matches the length of the pillow front, not including the button flap. BO kwise.

Pompoms

Make 4 pompoms as per instructions on page 155.

Finishing

Weave in all ends.

Side Seams

With WS together, fold the pillow into an envelope shape at the lower turning ridge and pin into place. To sew side seams, thread a tapestry needle with a length of color A. Starting at the lower turning ridge, insert needle into the bottom loop of the first selvedge stitch of pillow front and then into the top loop of corresponding purl stitch on pillow back. Continue working back and forth, from the bottom up to the CO edge of the pillow. Leave the button flap of the pillow open to be sewn later.

Felting and Blocking

Felt and block the pillow as instructed on page 160.

Assembly

Embellish the back of the pillow by sewing decorative buttons, evenly spaced, across flap. Stuff the pillow with wool fleece or Polyfil. Fold the flap down so that it covers the CO edge and pin into place. Using a sewing needle and thread, sew flap to pillow back along side seams and across the CO edge. Sew one pompom to each pillow corner.

Robin Hood

idding the world of injustice, defending the weak, and camping in Sherwood Forest with his band of merry men … it's no wonder that Robin Hood is such a beloved storybook character. This Prince of Thieves is the ultimate kid hero. He is a mischievous trickster with a truly noble spirit. In his world a child can play the champion and the villain at the same time. Clad in this dashing tunic and armed with imagination, your little lad or lass will be all set to defend the good people of Nottingham.

Tunic

This tunic is worked in a subtle slip stitch rib with a center placket and garter stitch hood. French knots and garter stitch bands embellish the hem and sleeves of this handsome sweater. This pattern is worked in the round from the hem to armholes and in rows from armhole to shoulder. The sleeves are worked from armhole to cuff in the round. A rustic braid, laced up the front placket, completes the medieval look of this garment.

SIZES

12 months (2 years, 4 years, 6 years, 8 years)

FINISHED MEASUREMENTS

Chest: 25 (27, 28, 30, 32)" [64 (69, 71, 76, 81)cm]
Length from shoulder to hem: 14½ (16, 18½, 20, 21)" [37 (41, 47, 51, 53)cm]

Sample size 8

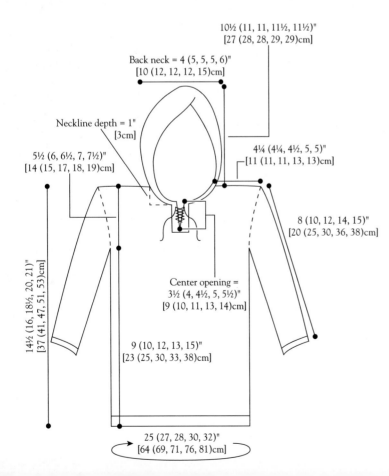

10½ (11, 11, 11½, 11½)"
[27 (28, 28, 29, 29)cm]

Back neck = 4 (5, 5, 5, 6)"
[10 (12, 12, 12, 15)cm]

Neckline depth = 1"
[3cm]

5½ (6, 6½, 7, 7½)"
[14 (15, 17, 18, 19)cm]

4¼ (4¼, 4½, 5, 5)"
[11 (11, 11, 13, 13)cm]

8 (10, 12, 14, 15)"
[20 (25, 30, 36, 38)cm]

14½ (16, 18½, 20, 21)"
[37 (41, 47, 51, 53)cm]

Center opening =
3½ (4, 4½, 5, 5½)"
[9 (10, 11, 13, 14)cm]

9 (10, 12, 13, 15)"
[23 (25, 30, 33, 38)cm]

25 (27, 28, 30, 32)"
[64 (69, 71, 76, 81)cm]

MATERIALS

Cascade Yarns 220 (100% Peruvian Highland wool; 220 yd. [201m] per 100 skein): #2445, Sherwood Forest (color A), 3 (4, 4, 5, 5) skeins; #9465, Black Sheep (color B), 1 (1, 2, 2, 2) skeins
US 6 (4mm) 16" circular needle
US 6 (4mm) 24" circular needle
US 6 (4mm) double-pointed needles
US 7 (4.5mm) 16" circular needle
US 7 (4.5mm) 24" circular needle
US 7 (4.5mm) double-pointed needles
Stitch markers
Stitch holders
Tapestry needle
Row counter (optional)

GAUGE

18 sts and 26 rows = 4" (10cm) in St st on US 7 (4.5mm) needle, or size needed to obtain gauge

STITCH PATTERNS

Stockinette stitch worked in the round—Knit all stitches every round.
Garter stitch worked flat—Knit all stitches every row.
Garter stitch worked in the round—Knit a round, purl a round.
Slip stitch pattern worked in the round—Work all odd rounds: *k3, sl 1; rep from * to end. Knit all even rounds.
Slip stitch pattern worked flat—Work RS rows: *k3, sl 1; rep from * to end. Purl all WS rows.
K2tog (page 149)
P2tog (page 150)
Skpo (page 151)
Ssk (page 150)
Ssp (page 150)
M1 (page 149)
Yo (page 148)

SPECIAL TECHNIQUES

Three-needle bind-off (page 151)
French knots (page 156)
Four-strand braid (see instructions in this pattern)

Instructions

Tunic Border

With 24" US 6 needle and color B, CO 55 (59, 63, 67, 71) sts, pm, CO 57 (61, 65, 69, 73) sts—112 (120, 128, 136, 144) sts.

Place a contrasting marker and join in the round. Work in garter stitch for 8 rounds, slipping markers as you go. Cut yarn.

Tunic Body

Switch to color A and 24" US 7 needle and knit 1 round. Continue to slip the markers as you come to them.
Rnd 1: *K3, sl 1; rep from * to end.
Rnd 2: Knit.
Rnds 1 and 2 make up the patt stitch for the body up to the armholes. Repeat these 2 rounds until the piece measures 9 (10, 12, 13, 15)" [23 (25, 30, 33, 38)cm] from CO edge, ending with Rnd 2 of patt.

Divide for Front and Back

At this point the work will be divided for the front and back of the sweater. The remainder of the sweater body will be worked in established patt back and forth in rows. *K3, sl 1; rep from * 12 (13, 14, 15, 16) times, k3 to marker—55 (59, 63, 67, 71) sts. These stitches form the sweater front. Cut yarn or tuck the skein of yarn attached to these stitches into the body of the sweater for later use. Join a second skein of yarn after the marker, ssk, k2, *sl 1, k3; rep from * 11 (12, 13, 14, 15) times, end sl 1, k2, k2tog, ending at left armhole of the sweater back—55 (59, 63, 67, 71) sts. These stitches form the sweater back. Do not cut yarn.

Put the 55 (59, 63, 67, 71) sts from the first half of the round (the sweater front) on a holder to be worked after the back is complete.

Sweater Back

In this section, you will be working on the 55 (59, 63, 67, 71) sts for sweater back only.
Turn work so that the WS of sweater back is facing, work in patt below, beg at left armhole edge.

Next row (WS): Purl, ending at right armhole edge.
Next row (RS): K3, *sl 1, k3; rep from * 12 (13, 14, 15, 16) times.
Rep last two rows until piece measures 5½ (6, 6½, 7, 7½)" [14 (15, 17, 18, 19)cm] from the base of the armhole, ending with a WS row. Cut yarn.

Slip the stitches for the sweater back onto a holder or spare needle.

Sweater Front

Slip the 55 (59, 63, 67, 71) sts for sweater front onto 16" or 24" US 7 needle. Turn work so that the WS of the sweater front is facing. Beg at right front armhole and work in patt below.

Next row (WS): Purl.
Next row (RS): *K3, sl 1; rep from * 12 (13, 14, 15, 16) times, end k3.
Rep last two rows for 1 (1, 1, 1, 1½)" [3 (3, 3, 3, 4)cm], ending with a WS row. Do not cut yarn.

Divide for Neck Opening

In this section, stitches at the center of the sweater front will be BO for the placket. The placket will be added after the sweater front, shoulder seams, and sleeves are complete.

Preparatory row (RS): Beg at left armhole edge, work in established patt across 23 (25, 26, 28, 29) sts for left front, BO 9 (9, 11, 11, 13) sts for placket, work in patt to end of row for right front.
From here both right and left fronts will be worked simultaneously with separate skeins of yarn. You can choose to work the left and right front on two separate needles or use the same circular for both.
Next row (WS): Beg at right armhole edge, purl to the placket opening. Join a second skein of color A at the left front edge of placket and purl to the left armhole edge.
Next row (RS): Work in established patt to left front placket opening. Skip over placket stitches and pick up yarn for right front and work in patt to right armhole edge.
Rep last two rows until front measures 4½ (5, 5½, 6, 6½)" [11 (13, 14, 15, 17cm)] from beg of armhole opening, ending with a WS row.

Neckline Shaping

Row 1 (RS): Work in patt to 3 sts before left placket edge, k2tog, k1. At right placket edge, k1, ssk, work in patt to right armhole edge—22 (24, 25, 27, 28) sts each side of neck.

Row 2 (WS): P to last 3 sts of right front, ssp, p1. Move to left front, p1, p2tog, p to end of row—21 (23, 24, 26, 27) sts each side of neck.

Rep last two rows 2 times more—17 (19, 20, 22, 23) sts rem for each side of neck.

Continue to work in established patt without dec until fronts measure 5½ (6, 6½, 7, 7½)" [14 (15, 17, 18, 19)cm] from base of armhole and the fronts and back are equal in length, ending with a WS row. Cut yarn.

Shoulder Seams

Slide each set of shoulder stitches onto a separate US 6 dpns. Turn sweater inside out so that the RS of the sweater are together. With color A, and 16" US 6 needle, beg at right armhole edge with WS of sweater front facing. Work a three-needle bind-off across the right shoulder stitches. Do not fasten off last stitch, instead use it to begin binding off stitches for center back. BO 21 (21, 23, 23, 25) sts for back of the neck. Do not cut yarn. Continue across the row, working a three-needle bind-off across the rem stitches for the left shoulder ending at the left armhole edge. Cut yarn and fasten off.

Sleeves

The sleeves are worked in the round from the armhole edge to the cuff.

Beg at base of one armhole with RS facing, color B, and US 6 dpn. Pick up 54 (58, 64, 64, 72) sts around armhole edge, pm and arrange stitches evenly on dpns. Join work in the round.

Sleeve Trim
Rnd 1: Purl.
Rnd 2: Knit.
Rnds 3–6: Rep Rnds 1 and 2 twice more.
Rnd 7: Rep Rnd 1. Cut yarn.

Sleeve Body
Join color A, switch to US 7 dpns, and knit to end of round.
Dec Rnd: Ssk, k to within 2 sts of marker, k2tog, sm—52 (56, 62, 62, 70) sts.

Continue to knit the sleeve in St st, as established, working Dec Rnd every fourth round until 36 (38, 40, 42, 44) sts rem and sleeve measures 8 (10, 12, 14, 15)" [20 (25, 30, 36, 38)cm] from armhole edge. BO all rem sts.

Repeat for second sleeve.

Placket

To work the placket, you will pick up stitches around the center opening and work in garter stitch rows. Decreases, worked every other row, form the mitered corners at the base of the placket.

With RS of sweater facing, beg at the neck edge of left front opening and using color B and 16" US 6 needle, pick up 15 (17, 19, 22, 24) sts evenly down left front opening, pm at corner of left front and lower placket edge. Continuing on, pick up 10 (10, 12, 12, 14) sts along the base of the placket to the lower edge of the right front opening, pm. Pick up final 15 (17, 19, 22, 24) sts evenly along right front opening up to the right neckline—40 (44, 50, 56, 62) sts.

Row 1 (WS): Knit, slipping markers as you go.
Row 2 (RS): *K to within 2 sts of marker, skpo, sm, k2tog; rep from * once, k to end of row—36 (40, 46, 52, 58) sts.
Row 3: Knit.
Row 4 (Eyelet Row): K1 (1, 1, 2, 2), [ssk, yo, k2] 2 (3, 3, 4, 4) times, [ssk, yo] 1 (0, 1, 0, 1) time(s), k1, skpo, sm, k2tog, k4 (4, 6, 6, 8), skpo, sm, k2tog, k1 [yo, k2tog] 1 (0, 1, 0, 1) time(s), [k2, yo, k2tog] 2 (3, 3, 4, 4) times, end k1 (1, 1, 2, 2)—32 (36, 42, 48, 54) sts.
Rows 5 and 7: Knit.
Row 6: Rep Row 2—28 (32, 38, 44, 50) sts.
BO, working decreases at corners as in previous rows.

Hood

With color B, 24" US 6 needle, and RS facing, pick up 5 sts along right placket top. Pick up 6 (6, 7, 8, 8) sts evenly along right neckline, 23 (23, 25, 25, 27) sts along back of neck, and 6 (6, 7, 8, 8) sts along left front to left placket. Pick up an additional 5 sts along top of left placket—45 (45, 49, 51, 53) sts.

Beg at left front with WS facing, k22 (22, 24, 25, 26), pm, k1, pm, k22 (22, 24, 25, 26).

Work in garter stitch, knitting all rows and slipping markers, for 1" (3cm), ending with a WS row.

Next row (RS): Knit to marker, M1, sm, k1, sm, M1, k to end—47 (47, 51, 53, 55) sts.
Next row (WS): Knit.
Rep last two rows 10 times—67 (67, 71, 73, 75) sts.

Work in garter stitch without further shaping until hood measures 10½ (11, 11, 11½, 11½)" [27 (28, 28, 29, 29)cm] from neckline edge, ending with a WS row. Do not cut yarn.

Hood Seam
The seam is worked on the outside of the hood.
Beg at right hood front with RS facing, fold the hood in half so that the front edges and WS of work are together. Hold the circular needle so that the two ends of the needle are parallel to one another. Using a US 6 dpn as the working needle and beg at the front edge of the hood, work three-needle bind-off across all the stitches to the back of the hood. BO the last stitch (the one between the markers) after the last pair of stitches has been bound off. Cut yarn and fasten off.

Embellishing the Border and Sleeve Trim
Thread a tapestry needle with color A and embellish the hem and the sleeve trim by working French knots in the ditch formed between the second and third garter ridge. Space the knots evenly, working one knot for every fourth knitted stitch beginning and ending at a side seam for the hem and at the underarm for the sleeves.

Finishing
Weave in all ends.
Block sweater.

Placket Tie: Four-Strand Braid
Braid, ribbon, or leather cording are all attractive options for the placket tie.
The directions for making the four-strand braid used in the sample sweater follow.

Cut eight 72" (183cm) strands of color B. Hold the eight strands together and tie a knot at one end of the bundle. Divide the eight lengths of yarn into four groups with two lengths of yarn per group. From this point on the groups of yarn will be referred to as "strands."

Making a braid with four strands is similar to making a three-strand braid. Beg by holding two strands of yarn in each hand. Arrange the yarn so that there is one inside strand and one outside strand in each hand. To make the braid, the outside strands are alternately moved to the center position.

1. Bring the outside strand held in your right hand over the one next to it and into to the center position.
2. Now bring the outside strand in your left hand over the three center strands and place it between the center and outside strands in your right hand.
3. Bring the outside strand in your right hand between the center and outside strands in your left hand.
4. Repeat the above steps until the entire length of yarn is braided. Secure the end of the braid with a knot.

Thread tie through placket eyelets.

Crowns

Whether your child is pretending to be Prince Charming, King Arthur, Cinderella or the Queen of Hearts, a suitable crown is essential. Included here are three royally inspired designs. Fun and practical, these regal crowns are the perfect addition to your child's fairy tale and real world wardrobes.

Princess Crown

This crown can be made two different ways, as a hat for chilly days and as a circlet of gold for dress-up and play. By itself, this glittering crown makes a darling party hat for holiday celebrations, an ideal topper for your favorite birthday girl or boy, and is perfect for games of pretend. Fun and easy to knit, it provides the perfect last-minute gift. With lacey details and delicate picot trim, the hat is a unique blend of fashion and function that will please the most discriminating princess. Made in washable merino wool, this cozy hat will keep your little princess warm and feeling pretty all winter long.

King's Crown

This handsome crown is truly fit for a king. Knit in two tiers with embroidered embellishments, it is made with beautiful textured, worsted weight wool in rich jewel-tones. This imperial crown is substantial enough to keep your young prince warm on the coldest winter days. Although originally designed for the king of the castle, this colorful hat is so appealing that you will want to knit it for all the members of your court. Not just for royalty, you could also make it in bright colors, embellished with bobbles and beads for your favorite court jester.

Princess Crown

This hat is made in two sections: the hat body and the crown. Both are worked separately, in the round, from the top down. The body of the hat is worked first. Once it is complete the crown is worked on a separate needle. The two pieces are joined together by layering the crown on top of the hat and knitting them together as one. The hatband is worked last and is finished with a facing and hem. The crown, hatband, and facing are used to make the alternate version of this pattern.

SIZES
6–12 months (2–4 years, 4 years–small adult)

FINISHED MEASUREMENTS
The eyelet bands in the body of this hat make it very stretchy, so it will accommodate a wide range of sizes. The measurements below reflect each hat size with and without stretching.

Head circumference: $15\frac{1}{2}$–16 ($18\frac{1}{2}$–19, $21\frac{1}{2}$–22)" [39–41 (47–48, 54–56)cm]

Sample size 2–4 years

MATERIALS
Filatura di Crosa *Zara* (100% merino superwash wool; $136\frac{1}{2}$ yd. [125m] per 50g skein): Main Color (MC) #1784, Purple, 1 (2, 2) skeins; Filatura di Crosa *New Smoking* (65% viscose, 35% polyester; 132 yd. [120m] per 25g skein: Contrast Color (CC) #01 Gold, 1 (2, 2) skeins

US 4 (3.5mm) 16" circular needle

US 4 (3.5mm) double-pointed needles

US 5 (3.75mm) 16" circular needle

Row counter

Stitch markers

Tapestry needle

GAUGE
22 sts and 29 rows = 4" (10cm) in St st with MC on US 4 (3.5mm) needle, or size needed to obtain gauge

20 sts and 40 rows = 4" (10cm) in garter stitch with CC on US 5 (3.75 mm) needle, or size needed to obtain gauge

STITCH PATTERNS
Stockinette stitch worked in the round—Knit all stitches every round.

Garter stitch worked in the round—Knit a round, purl a round.

K2tog (page 149)

Sk2po (page 151)

Sp2po (page 151)

Ssk (page 150)

Yo (page 148)

Instructions
Hat

With MC and US 4 dpns, CO 8 sts. Divide the stitches evenly on four needles. Join in the round, taking care not to twist stitches.

Top Shaping

You will begin with 2 sts on each dpn, using a fifth dpn as the working needle. Keep the stitches arranged evenly on the four dpns until you work through Rnd 8 and place the markers on Rnd 9. Once the markers are in place, you can move the stitches to the 16" US 4 circular needle, if desired.

Rnd 1: *K1, yo, k1; rep from * to end—12 sts.

Rnd 2 and all even rounds through Rnd 18 (22, 26): Knit.

Rnd 3: *K1, yo, k1, yo, k1; rep from * to end—20 sts.

Rnd 5: *K1, yo, k3, yo, k1; rep from * to end—28 sts.

Rnd 7: *K1, yo, k5, yo, k1; rep from * to end—36 sts.

Rnd 9: *Yo, pm, k9, pm; rep from * to end, placing a contrasting marker at the end of round—40 sts.

Rnd 11: *Yo, k1, yo, sm, k9, sm; rep from * to end—48 sts.

Rnd 13: *Yo, k to marker, yo, sm, k9, sm; rep from * to end—56 sts.

Rnds 15 and 17: Rep Rnd 13—72 sts.

NOTE: For 6–12 months size skip to Rnd 1 of Hat Body after completing Rnd 18.

For two largest sizes only:
Rnds 19 and 21: Rep Rnd 13—88 sts.
Rnds 20 and 22: Knit.

NOTE: For 2–4 years size skip to Rnd 1 of Hat Body after completing Rnd 22.

For largest size only:
Rnds 23 and 25: Rep Rnd 13—104 sts.
Rnds 24 and 26: Knit.

Hat Body

The stitch count from the previous section is maintained throughout the following eight rounds—72 (88, 104) sts.

Rnd 1: *Yo, k9 (13, 17), yo, sm, ssk, k5, k2tog, sm; rep from * to end.
Rnd 2 and all even rnds: Knit.

Rnd 3: *Yo, k11 (15, 19), yo, sm, ssk, k3, k2tog, sm; rep from * to end.
Rnd 5: *Yo, k13 (17, 21), yo, sm, ssk, k1, k2tog, sm; rep from * to end.
Rnd 7: *Yo, k15 (19, 23), yo, sm, sk2po, sm; rep from * to end.
Rnd 9: *Yo, k17 (21, 25), yo, sm, k1, sm; rep from * to end—80 (96, 112) sts.
Rem odd rnds: *Yo, ssk, k15 (19, 23), k2tog, yo, sm, k1, sm; rep from * to end—80 (96, 112) sts.

Continue in patt until piece measures 6½ (7, 8)" [17 (18, 20)cm] from top of hat, ending with an even round. Do not cut yarn; you will use it to join the hat and the crown together. Put the hat aside and work the crown.

Crown

With 16" US 5 needle and CC, CO 96 (112, 128) sts. Join work in the round.
Rnd 1: Knit, placing a marker every 12 (14, 16) sts and placing a contrasting marker at the end of the round.
Rnd 2: *Yo, p4 (5, 6), sp2po, p4 (5, 6), yo, p1, sm; rep from * to end.
Rnd 3: Knit.
Rnds 4–11 (4–15, 4–19): Rep last two rounds 4 (6, 8) times.
Rnd 12 (16, 20): This is a dec rnd, *p4 (5, 6), sp2po, p4 (5, 6), p1, sm; rep from * to end—80 (96, 112) sts.
Rnd 13 (17, 21): Knit.
Rnd 14 (18, 22): Purl.
Rem rnds: Rep last two rounds 1 (2, 2) time(s). Do not cut yarn.

Join the Hat and Crown

Place the crown over the hat so that the RS of both pieces are facing you, the first stitch of the Hat Body and Crown are lined up together, and the needles are parallel to one another. With 16" US 4 needle and the MC, knit the two pieces together by inserting the RH needle into the first stitch of both the crown and the hat at the same time. Knit these 2 sts together as if they were a single stitch. Rep for all stitches on the two needles.

Hat Band

Rnd 1: Continuing with MC and US 4 needle, purl.

Rnd 2: With CC, *k1, sl 1 wyib; rep from * to end.

Rnd 3: With CC, *p1, sl 1 wyib; rep from * to end. Cut CC, leaving a long tail for weaving in later. The remainder of the hat will be worked with MC.

Rnds 4, 6, and 7: Knit.

Rnd 5: Purl.

Rnd 8: *K2tog, yo; rep from * to end. This round forms the picot edge of the hatband.

Rnds 9–14: Knit. These rounds form the facing of the hat edging.
BO.

Finishing

Weave in ends. Turn the facing to the inside of the hat along the picot edge and sew in place.

Because of the lacey shaping at the top of the hat, you will need to block the hat over a hat form. If you don't have a hat form you can make your own by stuffing a plastic bag with paper and/or plastic bags. Stuff and shape the form to the size needed and seal it with tape. Wash or mist the hat with warm water. Put the hat over the form, leaving it there until it is completely dry.

Alternate Version

Sometimes you need a crown to be just a crown. To make the crown without the hat, work the Crown section of the pattern followed by the Hat Band section of the pattern. The hat band and facing give the crown body and make it soft and comfy against the skin.

King's Crown

This hat is made in the round from the top down. The triangle points of the crown are worked separately in garter stitch rows and are knitted to the hat one at a time. The two tiers of the hat are bordered by bands of reverse stockinette stitch and a hatband of attached I-cord.

SIZES
12–24 months, (2–4 years, 4 years–small adult)

FINISHED MEASUREMENTS
Head circumference: 19 (20$^{1}/_{2}$, 21$^{3}/_{4}$)" [48 (52, 55)cm]

Sample size 2–4 years

MATERIALS
Manos del Uruguay *Wool Classica* (100% Corriedale and merino wool blend; 138 yd. [126m] per 100g skein): #36 Mallard (color A), 1 skein; #115 Flame (color B), 1 skein; X Topaz (color C), 1 skein; #55 Olive (color D), 1 skein
US 8 (5mm) 16" circular needle
US 8 (5mm) double-pointed needles
Row counter
Stitch markers
Tapestry needle
Cardboard circle, 8" (20cm) diameter

NOTE: Each hat requires approximately 100–200 yd. (91–183m) of yarn. The yarn previously mentioned will yield three to four hats of varying colorways.

GAUGE

14 sts and 24 rows = 4" (10cm) in St st on US 8 (5mm) needle, or size needed to obtain gauge

STITCH PATTERNS

Stockinette stitch worked in the round—Knit all stitches every round.
Garter stitch worked flat—Knit all stitches every row.
Reverse stockinette stitch worked in the round—Purl all stitches every round.
I-cord (page 155)
K2tog (page 149)
Kfb (page 148)
Yo (page 148)

SPECIAL TECHNIQUES

Attached I-cord (see instructions in this pattern)
French knots (page 156)

Instructions
Hat Top

With color A and dpns, CO 6 sts. Divide the stitches evenly over three dpns and join in the round.

Rnd 1: *Yo, k1, pm; rep from * around placing a contrasting marker at end of round—12 sts.
Rnd 2: Knit, slipping markers as you go.
Rnd 3: *Yo, k to marker, sm; rep from * to end of round—18 sts.
Rnds 4–23 (4–25, 4–27): Rep last two rounds 10 (11, 12) times moving to the 16" needle when stitches become crowded—78 (84, 90) sts.
Rnd 24 (26, 28): Knit.

Do not cut yarn. You will drop color A to work the reverse St st band and pick it up again after the band is complete.

Reverse Stockinette Stitch Band 1

With color B, knit 1 round and purl 4 rounds. Cut yarn.

Hat Body Section 1

Knit 8 rounds with color A. Do not cut yarn.
Put the hat aside while you make the triangles for this section of the hat.

Triangles

The six triangles forming the crown of the hat are worked back and forth in rows on dpns.

CO 2 sts using color C.
Row 1: Knit.
Row 2: Kfb, k to end—3 sts.
Rows 3–12 (3–13, 3–14): Rep row 2—13 (14, 15) sts.
Knit 3 more rows without increasing. Cut yarn, leaving a long tail for weaving in later.

Make five more triangles as above. You should be able to fit two to three triangles on a dpn. Use additional dpns as necessary.

NOTE: Here is a trick to keep all of your triangles facing the same direction. For triangles with an odd number of stitches, turn the work before casting on the next triangle and cast on at the opposite end of the needle (the tail from the last triangle made will be trailing from the left edge of the work). For triangles with an even number of stitches, do not turn work, instead push the triangle just completed down the needle and cast on the next triangle beside it (the tail from the previous triangle will be trailing off the right edge of the triangle).

After six triangles are complete, arrange them on the dpns so that all of the triangles are facing the same way and the tails are trailing off the same side of each triangle.

Attach the Triangles

Knit the triangles to the hat by placing the needle holding the triangles on top of the hat so that the needles are parallel to one another, the RS of the hat is facing you and

the tails are trailing off the RH side of each triangle. With color B and using the circular needle as the working needle, knit the first triangle stitch and the first hat stitch together by inserting the RH needle into both stitches at the same time and knitting them as one, moving the tails of the triangles to the back of the work, between the two needles, and weaving them in as you go. Rep for all of the triangle and hat stitches.

Reverse Stockinette Stitch Band 2

Continuing with color B, purl 4 rounds. Cut yarn.

Hat Body Section 2

Join color A and work the next 8 rounds as follows:
Rnd 1: Knit.
Rnd 2: *K2tog, k11 (12, 13), sm; rep from * around—72 (78, 84) sts.
Rnds 3–6: Knit.
Rnd 7: *K2tog, k10 (11, 12), sm; rep from * around—66 (72, 78) sts.
Rnd 8: Knit.
Put the hat aside while you make the second set of triangles.

Second Set of Triangles

You will make the second set of triangles like the first but end with a different stitch count.

Using color C, make six triangles with 11 (12, 13) sts each. Finish each triangle like those in the first set, by knitting the last 3 rows without increasing.

Attach the Triangles

The placement of this set of triangles is staggered with the first set. Each new triangle is attached to the hat so that it is centered between two triangles from the first set. To do this you will need to slip hat stitches and reassign the beg of the round. Slip the first 5 (6, 7) hat stitches (at the beg of the round) from the LH to the RH needle. Place a marker at this spot. This is the beg of the round for the remainder of the hat. Beginning at this spot and using color B, knit the second set of triangles to the hat as you did the first set. After the last triangle has been attached, sm and purl a round with color B (beg and ending at the new beginning of the round). Cut yarn.

Attach the I-Cord Hatband

With color A and dpns, CO 4 sts. *K4, do not turn work. Slide stitches to opposite end of the dpn and knit across. This joins the I-cord in the round. Rep from * for 3 rounds.

To attach the I-cord to the hat, knit the first 3 sts of the next I-cord round, pick up the hat (with RS facing) and hold the dpn with the rem I-cord stitch parallel and in front of the needle holding the hat stitches. Insert the working dpn (the one holding the 3 I-cord sts) into both the rem I-cord stitch and the first hat stitch. Knit these 2 sts together as if they were one. You now have 4 sts on one dpn. Slide the 4 sts to the opposite end of the needle. The second dpn is empty. Using the empty dpn, knit 3 sts of I-cord and then knit the fourth I-cord st and the next hat stitch together. Continue in this way, working the first 3 sts of I-cord plain and knitting the fourth I-cord stitch to the hat until all stitches have been worked.

BO rem I-cord stitches. Cut yarn and fasten off final stitch. Sew BO and CO edges of I-cord together at the inside of the hat.

Embellish the Reverse Stockinette Stitch Bands

Thread a tapestry needle with color D. Embroider French knots along the center of the reverse St st bands. Space them evenly, making one knot for every fourth knitted stitch.

Finishing

Weave in all ends. To block hat, cut an 8" (20cm) circle out of cardboard. Place the cardboard round inside a plastic bag. Wash or mist the hat with warm water. Put the hat over the piece of cardboard so that the cardboard round is nestled inside the uppermost band. Loosely stuff the hat body with plastic bags and air dry.

NOTE: You can also use purchased cardboard cake rounds for hat blocking. They can be found in the cake decorating section of most craft stores and come in a variety of diameters.

Renaissance Man

This elegant tunic is perfect for pages and princes alike. It is a modern interpretation of Renaissance garb and was originally designed for my own castle-loving son. Made with simple lines and princely details, this sweater allows young knights to quest in comfort and style. It is knit in sensible washable wool, making it the perfect outfit for charging about the kingdom and for holding court.

Tunic

This sweater is worked from the hem up, beginning with the crenellated border. The border is made up of eight separate rectangles. Once all eight rectangles have been made, they are knitted together and joined in the round. The sweater is worked in the round up to the armholes and in rows from the armholes to the shoulders. The sleeves of the sweater are worked in the round from the armhole edge down, and are trimmed with a cuff design that mimics the hem of the sweater.

SIZES
2 years (4 years, 6 years, 8 years)

FINISHED MEASUREMENTS
Chest: 28 (30, 32, 34)" [71 (76, 81, 86)cm]
Shoulder to hem: 18$^{1}/_{2}$ (20, 21$^{1}/_{2}$, 23)" [47 (51, 55, 58)cm]

Sample size 4 years

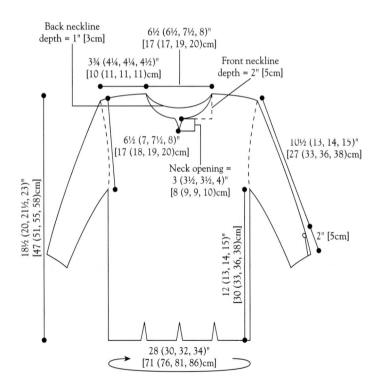

Back neckline depth = 1" [3cm]

6½ (6½, 7½, 8)" [17 (17, 19, 20)cm]

3¾ (4¼, 4¼, 4½)" [10 (11, 11, 11)cm]

Front neckline depth = 2" [5cm]

6½ (7, 7½, 8)" [17 (18, 19, 20)cm]

10½ (13, 14, 15)" [27 (33, 36, 38)cm]

Neck opening = 3 (3½, 3½, 4)" [8 (9, 9, 10)cm]

18½ (20, 21½, 23)" [47 (51, 55, 58)cm]

12 (13, 14, 15)" [30 (33, 36, 38)cm]

2" [5cm]

28 (30, 32, 34)" [71 (76, 81, 86)cm]

MATERIALS
Cascade Yarns *220 Superwash* (100% superwash wool; 220 yd. [201m] per 100g skein): #856 Teal, 4 (4, 5, 6) skeins
US 6 (4mm) 16" circular needle
US 6 (4mm) 24" circular needle
US 6 (4mm) double-pointed needles
US 7 (4.5mm) 16" circular needle
US 7 (4.5mm) 24" circular needle
US 7 (4.5mm) double-pointed needles
US size F (3.75mm) crochet hook
Stitch markers
Stitch holders
Tapestry needle
Row counter
$^{1}/_{2}$" (1cm) buttons—2
$^{3}/_{4}$" (2cm) buttons—2
1" (3cm) buttons—8
Sewing needle
Sewing thread to match yarn

GAUGE
18 sts and 24 rows = 4" (10cm) in St st on US 7 (4.5mm) needle, or size needed to obtain gauge

STITCH PATTERNS
Garter stitch worked flat—Knit all stitches every row.
Garter stitch worked in the round—Knit a round, purl a round.
Crochet chain stitch—Worked with 1 st already on crochet hook, wrap yarn around hook from back to front, and pull the resulting loop through the stitch on the crochet hook.
K2tog (page 149)
Skpo (page 151)
Ssk (page 150)

SPECIAL TECHNIQUES
Three-needle bind-off (page 151)
Crochet bind-off (see instruction in this pattern.)

Instructions
Tunic Hem
Rectangle Tabs
With 24" US 6 needle, CO 16 (17, 18, 19) sts.
Rows 1–7: Knit.
Change to 24" US 7 needle.
Row 8 (WS): K4 (4, 5, 5), p8 (9, 8, 9), k4 (4, 5, 5).

Row 9: Knit.
Rows 10–19: Rep Rows 8 and 9.
Row 20: Rep Row 8.

Cut yarn, leaving the finished rectangle on the needle. Rep rectangle instructions seven times for a total of eight rectangles.

Join the Rectangle Tabs

Once all eight rectangles are complete, arrange them so that the tail of each rectangle trails off the RH edge of the work when the right side of the work is facing.

With RS facing and 24" US 7 needle, knit across four rectangles, connecting them to one another, pm and knit across rem four rectangles—128 (136, 144, 152) sts. Place a contrasting marker and join in the round, being careful not to twist stitches.

Sweater Border

In this section, you will beg working in the round, slipping markers as you go.
Rnd 1: *P4 (4, 5, 5), k8 (9, 8, 9), p4 (4, 5, 5); rep from * to end.
Rnd 2: Knit.
Rnds 3–16: Rep Rnds 1 and 2.
Rnd 17: *P3, k10 (11, 12, 13), p3; rep from * to end.
Rnd 18: Knit.
Rnds 19–22: Rep Rnds 17 and 18.

Sweater Body

The next two rounds establish the stitch patt for the sweater body.
Rnd 1: P1, k14 (15, 16, 17), *p2, k14 (15, 16, 17); rep from * to last st, p1.
Rnd 2: Knit.

Rep Rnds 1 and 2 until work measures 12 (13, 14, 15)" [30 (33, 36, 38)cm] from CO edge of rectangles, ending with Rnd 1.

Divide for Front and Back

K64 (68, 72, 76), sm, k64 (68, 72, 76). Put last 64 (68, 72, 76) sts on a holder or spare needle to be held in reserve for the front of the sweater. Cut yarn, leaving a long tail for weaving in later.

From this point on the sweater body will be worked back and forth in rows in the patt established in the previous Sweater Body section. To do this, work odd rows as for Rnd 1 of the Sweater Body, purling the stitches that you purled in previous odd rounds. On the even rows, purl all stitches.

Sweater Back
Armhole Shaping

Row 1 (RS): Join yarn at right armhole edge with the RS of work facing. Working on the sweater back only, BO 2 (2, 3, 3) sts kwise for right armhole, work in patt as established for sweater body (Rnd 1), ending at left armhole—62 (66, 69, 73) sts.
Row 2: Beg at left armhole, BO 2 (2, 3, 3) sts pwise, p to end—60 (64, 66, 70) sts.
Row 3: Ssk, work in patt to last 2 sts, k2tog—58 (62, 64, 68) sts.
Row 4: Purl.
Rows 5–8: Rep Rows 3 and 4—54 (58, 60, 64) sts.

Continue in patt without further shaping until armhole measures 5 (5½, 6, 6½)" [13 (14, 15, 17)cm], ending with a WS row.

Back Neckline Shaping

The shaping for the right and left neckline is worked at the same time. A second skein of yarn is introduced for the back of the neck and the left shoulder. On each row, you will work one shoulder with one skein and the other shoulder with a second skein. You can choose to work the shoulders on two separate needles or use the same circular for both shoulders.

Row 1 (RS): Work in patt for 17 (19, 20, 22) sts, k2tog. These stitches form the right shoulder. Join a second skein of yarn and work in patt across the next 16 sts for the back of the neck. Ssk, work in patt to end of row for the left shoulder.
Row 2: P18 (20, 21, 23), put the center 16 sts on a holder for the back of the neck. Pick up the yarn for the right shoulder and p18 (20, 21, 23).
Row 3: Work 16 (18, 19, 21) sts in patt, k2tog. Move to left shoulder, ssk, work rem 16 (18, 19, 21) sts in patt.
Row 4: P17 (19, 20, 22) for left and right shoulders.
Row 5 (for sizes 6 and 8 only): Work in patt to last 2 sts of right shoulder, k2tog. Move to left shoulder, ssk, work in patt to end of row.

You should now have 17 (19, 19, 21) sts on each needle.
Rem rows: Continue to work in established patt without further shaping until the piece measures 18½ (20, 21½, 23)" [47 (50, 55, 58)cm] from the CO edge of tunic hem, ending with a RS row.
Cut yarn and put shoulder stitches on holders.

Sweater Front
Armhole Shaping
Slip 64 (68, 72, 76) sts on reserve for sweater front onto the 24" US 7 needle. Join a new skein of yarn at the left underarm of the sweater front. Beg with RS facing, work Rows 1–8 of armhole shaping as for sweater back. Continue without further shaping until work measures 1½ (1½, 2, 2)" [4 (4, 5, 5)cm] from the base of the armhole edge, ending with a WS row.

Divide for Sweater Front Opening

In this section, you will divide the stitches for the front opening. The center 6 sts of the sweater front form the base of the center placket. The right and left sides of the front opening are worked over the rem stitches.

The left side of the center opening is worked first. After working across the stitches on Row 1 of Left Front, place the stitches for the center placket and the right front onto a holder to be worked later. Continue, working on the stitches

for the left front only. After the left front is complete, put the left front stitches onto a holder and slide the stitches for the right front onto the needle and work the right front. The 6 sts for the center placket will remain on the original holder to be worked later.

Left Front
Row 1 (RS): Beg at left armhole edge, work in patt for 24 (26, 27, 29) sts, turn.
Put rem stitches on a holder for the center placket and right front, and continue to work on the left front.
Row 2: P24 (26, 27, 29) sts to left armhole.
Continue working in patt until left armhole measures 4½ (5, 5½, 6)" [11 (13, 14, 15)cm], ending with a WS row.

Left Front Neckline Shaping
Row 1 (RS): Work in patt to neck edge.
Row 2: BO 4 (4, 5, 5) sts pwise, p to end—20 (22, 22, 24) sts.
Row 3: Work in patt to last 2 sts, k2tog—19 (21, 21, 23) sts.
Row 4: Purl.
Rows 5–8: Rep Rows 3 and 4—17 (19, 19, 21) sts.

Continue to work in patt without further shaping until left front and back are of equal length, ending with a RS row. Cut yarn and slide the stitches for the left front shoulder onto a holder.

Right Front
Transfer the stitches for the right front onto the 24" US 7 needle, leaving the 6 sts on reserve for the center placket on the holder.

Join a new skein of yarn at the right front neck opening, with RS facing, work in patt across rem 24 (26, 27, 29) sts to right armhole.

Work as for left front in established patt until armhole measures 4½ (5, 5½, 6)" [11 (13, 14, 15)cm], ending with a WS row.

Right Front Neckline Shaping
Row 1 (RS): BO 4 (4, 5, 5) sts kwise at neck opening, work in patt to end of row—20 (22, 22, 24) sts.

Row 2: Beg at armhole, purl.
Row 3: Ssk, k18, (20, 20, 22), work in patt to end of row—19 (21, 21, 23) sts.
Row 4: Purl.
Rows 5–8: Rep Rows 3 and 4—17 (19, 19, 21) sts.

Continue to work in patt as for left front until right front measures same as right back, ending with a RS row. Cut yarn.

Shoulder Seams

Slide each set of shoulder stitches onto a separate US 6 dpn. Turn the sweater inside out so that RS of the sweater are together. With WS facing and beginning at the armhole edge, join yarn and work a three-needle bind-off to join the front and back stitches of one shoulder together. Cut yarn and fasten off.

Rep for second shoulder, working from the armhole to the neck edge.

Sleeves

With US 6 dpns, RS facing, and beg at base of one armhole, pick up 58 (62, 68, 72) sts around armhole edge. Place a marker, arrange stitches evenly on dpns, and join work in the round.

Rnd 1: Knit.
Change to US 7 dpns.
Rnds 2–5: Knit.
Rnd 6: K1, ssk, k to last 3 sts, k2tog, k1—56 (60, 66, 70) sts.
Rnds 7–50 (7–56, 7–62, 7–68): Rep Rnds 1–6 above, 7 (8, 9, 10) times—42 (44, 48, 50) sts.

Cuff
Rnd 1: K18 (19, 21, 22), p6, k18 (19, 21, 22).
Rnd 2 and all even rnds: Knit.
Rnd 3: Rep Rnd 1.
Rnd 5: K1, ssk, k15 (16, 18, 19), p6, k15 (16, 18, 19), k2tog, k1—40 (42, 46, 48) sts.
Rnd 7: K17 (18, 20, 21), p6, k17 (18, 20, 21).

Rnd 9: K16 (17, 19, 20), p8, k16 (17, 19, 20).
Rnd 11: K1, ssk, k13 (14, 16, 17), p8, k13 (14, 16, 17), k2tog, k1—38 (40, 44, 46) sts.
Rnds 13, 15, 17, 19, 21, and 23: K15 (16, 18, 19), p8, k15 (16, 18, 19).

From this point on, the cuff will be worked back and forth in rows to create the center opening. As you work through the following rows you will continue to slip the marker from the previous rounds.

Set-up Row: K19 (20, 22, 23), turn.
Row 1 (WS): K4, p15 (16, 18, 19), sm, p19 (20, 22, 23).
Row 2: P4, k15 (16, 18, 19), sm, k19 (20, 22, 23).
Rows 3–6: Rep Rows 1 and 2.
Row 7 (WS): K19 (20, 22, 23), sm, p19 (20, 22, 23).
Row 8: P19 (20, 22, 23), sm, k19 (20, 22, 23).
Rows 9–14: Rep Rows 7 and 8.
Row 15: BO 19 (20, 22, 23) kwise, sm, p19 (20, 22, 23).
Row 16: BO 19 (20, 22, 23) pwise to marker, cut yarn and fasten off.

Repeat for second sleeve.

Neck Trim

With RS facing, 16" US 6 needle, and beg at right front neck opening, pick up 16 (16, 18, 18) sts around right neck edge, knit across the 16 sts on hold for back neckline, and pick up 16 (16, 18, 18) sts around left neckline—48 (48, 52, 52) sts.

Knit 5 rows and BO.

Placket

With US 6 dpn, RS facing, and beg at upper-left front neckline edge, pick up 18 (21, 21, 24) sts along the left front opening down to the stitches on hold for the center placket. With a second dpn, knit across the 6 sts on reserve for the center front. With the third dpn, pick up 18 (21, 21, 24) sts along the right front opening, ending at the right front neckline edge—42 (48, 48, 54) sts.

Keep the stitches for the left, center, and right placket edges each on a separate dpn, working across each one with the fourth dpn.

Rows 1, 3, and 5 (WS): Knit.
Row 2 (RS): K16 (19, 19, 22), skpo (1st dpn), k2tog, k2, skpo (2nd dpn), k2tog, k16 (19, 19, 22) (3rd dpn)—38, (44, 44, 50) sts.
Row 4: K15 (18, 18, 21), skpo, k2tog, skpo, k2tog, k15 (18, 18, 21)—34 (40, 40, 46) sts.
Do not cut yarn after Row 5.

Crochet Bind-Off and Buttonholes

The buttonholes and placket edge are completed with a crochet bind-off. This bind-off is identical to a regular bind-off except that a crochet hook is held in the right hand instead of a knitting needle.

To work this bind-off, you will insert the crochet hook into the front of the stitch on the knitting needle, wrap yarn around the hook as if to knit, and draw the loop through the stitch and off the LH needle. *Insert hook into next stitch on the LH needle, wrap yarn around hook as before, drawing the loop through the stitch. You now have 2 sts on the crochet hook. Pull the second stitch worked through the first stitch—1 st rem on hook. Rep from *.

With RS facing and beg at the upper edge of the left neckline opening, BO 4 (5, 5, 6) sts in this manner, chain 2 sts, BO 5 (6, 6, 7) sts, chain 2 sts, BO 4 (5, 5, 6) sts, [BO2tog] 3 times, BO rem stitches for right front opening. Cut yarn and fasten off.

Finishing

Weave in all ends. Block sweater. Sew a 1" (3cm) button to the center of each rectangle of the tunic border. Center a ¾" (2cm) button on each sleeve directly above the cuff opening (the section that was worked flat). Sew in place. Position the ½" (1cm) buttons on the right front placket, across from the crochet chain buttonholes, and sew into place.

Modern Chain Maille

Your knight in shining armor will love this attractive chain maille. It's perfect for a day of storming the castle and slaying dragons. Knit in soft, washable merino wool, this cozy sweater can go right into the washer after a day of defending the realm. Completely seamless and a quick knit, this fairy tale sweater is as much fun to make as it is to wear.

Sweater

This yoked sweater is worked on big needles with lofty merino wool and is a really quick knit. The body of the sweater is worked in the round from the hem to the underarms, at which point the sweater body is put aside and the sleeves are worked from the cuff up (also in the round). The sleeves are joined to the sweater body and the remainder of the work progresses in the round up to the center opening. The rest of the sweater, from the center opening to the neckline edge, is worked back and forth in rows. Three decrease rows shape the yoke and the sweater is finished with crocheted edging along the neckline and front openings.

SIZES

6–12 months (2–4 years, 4–6 years, 6–8 years)

FINISHED MEASUREMENTS

Chest: 24 (25, 28, 29)" [61 (64, 71, 74)cm]
Length from back neck to hem: 16 (18, 19, 21)" [41 (46, 48, 53)cm]

Sample size 4–6 years

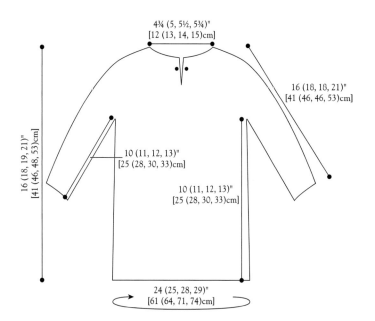

4¾ (5, 5½, 5¾)"
[12 (13, 14, 15)cm]

16 (18, 18, 21)"
[41 (46, 46, 53)cm]

16 (18, 19, 21)"
[41 (46, 48, 53)cm]

10 (11, 12, 13)"
[25 (28, 30, 33)cm]

10 (11, 12, 13)"
[25 (28, 30, 33)cm]

24 (25, 28, 29)"
[61 (64, 71, 74)cm]

MATERIALS

Tahki/Stacy Charles *Torino Bulky* (100% extra-fine merino wool; 55 yd. [50m] per 50g skein): # 236 Charcoal Grey, 7 (7, 8, 9) skeins
US 10 (6mm) 24" circular needle
US 10 (6mm) 12" circular needle
US 10 (6mm) double-pointed needle
US size I (5.5mm) crochet hook
Row counter
Stitch markers
Stitch holders
Tapestry needle
Decorative metal clasp
Sewing needle
Sewing thread to match yarn

GAUGE

12 sts and 20 rows = 4" (10cm) in Chain Maille Stitch on US 10 (6mm) needle, or size needed to obtain gauge

STITCH PATTERNS

Chain Maille Stitch worked in the round—*Purl 1 round, knit the following 2 rounds; rep from *.
K2tog (page 149)

SPECIAL TECHNIQUES

Single crochet (see the instructions in this pattern)
Kitchener stitch (page 152)

Instructions

Sweater Body

Using 24" needle, CO 72 (76, 84, 88) sts, pm, and join work in the round, being careful not to twist stitches.

Work Chain Maille Stitch
Rnd 1: P36 (38, 42, 44) for sweater front, place a contrasting marker for right underarm, p36 (38, 42, 44) for sweater back.
Rnds 2 and 3: Knit.
Rep Rnds 1–3 of chain maille stitch until piece measures approximately 10 (11, 12, 13)" [25 (28, 30, 33)cm], ending with Rnd 3 of patt.

Final Rnd: P36 (38, 42, 44), sm, p3 (3, 4, 4). Slip the last 6 (6, 8, 8) sts worked, including the marker, onto a holder for the right underarm. Purl across rem 33 (35, 38, 40) sts of sweater back. Slip the 3 (3, 4, 4) sts on each side of the marker [6 (6, 8, 8) sts total], as well as the marker, onto a holder for the left underarm. Cut yarn, leaving a 10" (25cm) tail. Put the sweater body aside and make the sleeves.

Sleeves

Using dpns, CO 24 (26, 28, 30) sts, pm. Arrange stitches evenly on dpns, join in the round, and work in chain maille stitch patt until sleeve measures approximately 10 (11, 12, 13)" [25 (28, 30, 33)cm] ending with a purl round. Put the 3 (3, 4, 4) sts on each side of the marker on a holder. The 6 (6, 8, 8) sts placed on the holder form the sleeve underarm. Put rem 18 (20, 20, 22) sts on the 12" circular needle so you can use the dpns for the second sleeve. Cut yarn, leaving a 15" (38cm) tail.

Repeat for second sleeve.

Yoke

Join the Sleeves

The sleeves are joined to the body in one row. You will knit across the stitches for the left sleeve, the sweater front, the right sleeve, and the sweater back—one right after the other. At the end of this row, all of the stitches for the sweater yoke will be on the 24" needle and the work will be joined in the round.

Beg at left edge of sweater back with the RS of work facing, use the 24" needle holding the sweater stitches to k across the 18 (20, 20, 22) sts of one sleeve, pm, k across 30 (32, 34, 36) sts of sweater front, pm, pick up the second sleeve and k18 (20, 20, 22) sts for right sleeve, pm, end row by knitting across the 30 (32, 34, 36) sts for sweater back, place a contrasting marker—96 (104, 108, 116) sts.

The contrast marker indicates the beg of the round, which starts at the back left shoulder. The order of the stitches on the needle is left sleeve, marker, sweater front, marker, right sleeve, marker, sweater back, contrast marker.

Join work in the round.
Work the next 5 rounds in established patt, ending with a purl round. Cut yarn.

Divide for Front Opening

The remainder of the yoke is worked back and forth in rows from this point on, with the opening centered at the front neck.

Continuing with the same needle, slip 18 (20, 20, 22) sts (left sleeve), the marker, and the first 15 (16, 17, 18) sts of sweater front from the LH to the RH needle.

Row 1 (RS): Join yarn at center front, k15 (16, 17, 18) sts for right front, sm, k18 (20, 20, 22) for right sleeve, sm, k30 (32, 34, 36) for sweater back, sm, k18 (20, 20, 22) for left sleeve, sm, k15 (16, 17, 18) for left front, turn.
Rows 2, 3, and 4: Purl.
Rows 5 and 6: Knit.
The 6 rows above form the patt for the remainder of the yoke.

Yoke Shaping

Rows 1–10: Work in patt established above, ending with Row 4 of the six row patt repeat, a WS row.
For size 6–12 months only, work the first decrease row next across Row 11 as directed below.
For all rem sizes, continue to work in established patt ending with Row 4 of patt repeat, a WS row. Work first decrease row across Row 17 as specified for each size below.

First Decrease Row
Size 6–12 Months
Row 11 (RS): K1, *k1, k2tog; rep from *, end k2—65 sts.

Size 2–4 Years
Row 17 (RS): K2tog, *k1, k2tog; rep from * to end—69 sts.

Size 4–6 Years
Row 17 (RS): K1, *k1, k2tog; rep from *, end k2—73 sts.

Size 6–8 Years
Row 17 (RS): K2tog, *k1, k2tog; rep from * to end—77 sts.

For All Sizes

Continue to work in patt for 8 (8, 8, 11) rows, through Row 19 (25, 25, 28).

Work second decrease row as specified for each size.

Second Decrease Row

Size 6–12 Months

Row 20 (WS): P2tog, *p1, p2tog; rep from * to end—43 sts.

Size 2–4 Years

Row 26 (WS): P1, *p1, p2tog; rep from *, end p2—47 sts.

Size 4–6 Years

Row 26 (WS): *P1, p2tog; rep from *, end p1—49 sts.

Size 6–8 Years

Row 29 (RS): K2tog, *k1, k2tog; rep from * to end—51 sts.

For All Sizes

Continue to work in patt for 8 (8, 8, 11) rows, through Row 28 (34, 34, 40).

Work third decrease row as specified for each size.

Third Decrease Row

Size 6–12 Months

Row 29 (RS): *K1, k2tog; rep from *, end k1—29 sts.

Size 2–4 Years

Row 35 (RS): K2tog, *k1, k2tog; rep from * to end—31 sts.

Size 4–6 Years

Row 35 (RS): K1, *k2tog, k1; rep from * to end—33 sts.

Size 6–8 Years

Row 41 (RS): K1, *k1, k2tog; rep from *, end k2—35 sts.

Next row all sizes (WS)

Row 30 (36, 36, 42): Knit.
BO 29 (31, 33, 35) sts kwise.

Underarm Seams

Kitchener stitch, or grafting, is used to join the sleeves to the sweater body and to close the hole at the underarm edge. To graft the right sleeve to the sweater body, slide the stitches on hold for the right underarm body onto one dpn and the stitches on hold for the right sleeve onto a separate dpn. Thread a tapestry needle with the tail from the sleeve stitches. With RS of work facing, position the dpns so that they are parallel to one another and the tapestry needle threaded with the tail from the sleeve stitches is trailing off of the RH side of the work. Weave the sleeve and the body stitches together by working Kitchener stitch (see instructions on page 152).

Rep for left sleeve.

Edging

Beg at the center back with RS facing and with the crochet hook, work two rows of single crochet (see instructions below) around the neck edge. Work 1 crochet st for every BO stitch. At the left and right front openings you will be working into selvedge stitches, not BO stitches. Make sure that you work the same number of stitches on both right and left front openings. A ratio of 3 crochet sts for every 4 selvedge sts works well.

NOTE: For a complete discussion of crochet techniques, see page 158.

Single Crochet

Hold the crochet hook in your right hand and the working yarn in your left. With RS facing, insert the hook into an edge stitch at the center back neckline. Holding the working yarn at the back of the work, wrap the yarn over the hook, pull yarn through the edge stitch to the right side of the work. *Insert the hook into the next edge stitch, yo, pull yarn through the stitch, yo, and pull yarn through both loops on the hook. Rep from * around the left neck edge, down the left front opening, up the right front opening, across the right front and back neckline, to back center (where you started), turn.

With WS facing, chain 1 st (see page 158) and rep as above working from right to left around the neckline edge to the back center. Cut yarn and fasten off.

Finishing

Weave in all ends and block sweater.
Sew the clasp to the right and left front openings.

Knitting Abbreviations

ABBREVIATION	MEANING
beg	beginning
BO	bind off
CC	contrasting color
ch	chain
cm	centimeter(s)
CO	cast on
dec	decrease(s)/decreasing
dpn(s)	double-pointed needle(s)
g	grams
inc	increase(s)/increasing
k	knit
kfb	knit into the front and back
k tbl	Knit through the back loop
k2tog	knit two stitches together
k2tog tbl	knit two stitches together through the back loop
kwise	knitwise
LH	left hand
M1	make one
M1L	make one left
M1R	make one right
m	meter(s)
MB	make bobble
MC	main color
mm	millimeter(s)
oz	ounces
p	purl
patt	pattern
pm	place marker
psso	pass slipped stitch over
ptbl	Purl through the back loop

ABBREVIATION	MEANING
p2tog	purl two stitches together
p2tog tbl	Purl two stitches together through the back loop
p3tog	purl three stitches together
pwise	purlwise
rem	remain(ing)
rep	repeat
rnd(s)	round(s)
RH	right hand
RS	right side
sc	single crochet
sl	slip
sm	slip marker
sl st	slip stitch
skpo	slip, knit one, pass slipped stitch over
sk2po	slip, knit two stitches together, pass slipped stitch over
sm	slip marker
sp2po	slip, purl two stitches together, pass slipped stitch over
ssk	slip, slip, knit
ssp	slip, slip, purl
st(s)	stitch(es)
St st	stockinette stitch
tbl	through the back loop
tog	together
WS	wrong side
w&t	wrap and turn
wyib	with yarn in back
wyif	with yarn in front
yd.	yard(s)
yo	yarn over
*	repeat directions following * as directed

Basic Techniques

Casting On

Before you start knitting, you need to get the first row of stitches on your needle. This is called casting on. This book uses four different cast-on techniques, each one uniquely suited to the task at hand. They all have one thing in common—**the slipknot.**

1. Measure out a length of yarn as directed in the instructions for the cast-on method being used. Hold the tail of the yarn in your left hand.
2. Make a loop by crossing the yarn coming from the skein over the tail.
3. Hold the bottom of the loop (the overlapped end) between the thumb and forefinger of your left hand.

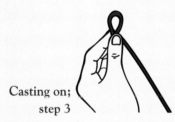

Casting on;
step 3

4. Reach into the loop with your right index finger and thumb, grab the yarn coming from the ball and pull it through the loop, thus creating a new loop.
5. Place the new loop onto your needle.
6. Tighten the loop by pulling on the tails so that it is securely on the needle and can slide across the needle easily.

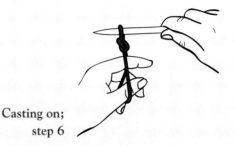

Casting on;
step 6

Long-Tail Cast-On

This is the cast-on used for most of the projects in this book. It makes a nice elastic edge and is a great all-purpose cast-on.

To begin this cast-on, you will need to know where to make the slipknot. Do this by multiplying the number of stitches needed by 1" (3cm) and adding two or three inches more.

1. Make a slipknot, leaving a tail equal to the measurement above.
   For example, if the pattern instructs you to "CO 10 sts" (cast on 10 stitches), you would make the slipknot 12–13" (30–33cm) from the end of the yarn.
2. Put the slipknot on your needle and hold the needle in your right hand. The slipknot is the first stitch of the cast-on row.
3. Bring your left thumb and index finger between the two strands hanging from the slipknot so that the tail is over the outside of your thumb and the yarn attached to the ball (the working yarn) is over the outside of your index finger. Use the remaining fingers of your left hand to hold the loose strands against your palm. Open up your left thumb and forefinger so that a V is formed from the two strands of the

slipknot. Use the index finger of your right hand to hold the slipknot in place on the needle.

4. With the palm of your left hand facing you, bring the needle toward your body. This creates a loop around your left thumb. Insert the tip of the needle under the thumb strand closest to you and come up through the loop on your thumb as shown.

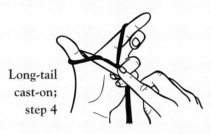

Long-tail cast-on; step 4

5. Rotate the wrist of your left hand toward your body so that your palm is facing down and place the strand on your index finger over the tip of the needle from front to back. Rotate your wrist back into the palm-up position.

6. Bring the tip of the needle from back to front through the loop on your thumb.

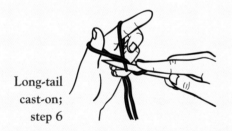

Long-tail cast-on; step 6

7. Still holding the yarn over your index finger and against your palm, remove your thumb from the loop. Place your thumb back under the working yarn and bring your thumb toward your body, gently tightening the new stitch on the needle.

8. You now have two stitches on your needle (the slipknot and the newly cast-on stitch). Repeat Steps 3–7 until you have the required number of stitches on the needle. Remember to keep the stitches tight enough so that they are secure but still slide easily on the needle.

Backward Loop Cast-On

This is the easiest and most basic cast-on. While this cast-on method is easy to learn, knitting from it and maintaining even tension on the first row of knitting can be tricky. I often use this cast-on when adding stitches to an existing row of knitting.

1. Make a slipknot about 6–10" (15–25cm) from the end of the yarn and place it on the needle. If you are working from an existing row of knitting, omit this step and move on to the following step.

2. Hold the needle in your right hand and the working yarn in your left hand. Make a loop in the working yarn as shown.

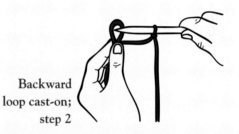

Backward loop cast-on; step 2

3. Place the loop onto the needle and tighten it by gently pulling on the working yarn. You now have two cast-on stitches on your needle (the slipknot and the newly made stitch).

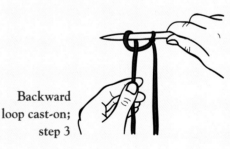

Backward loop cast-on; step 3

4. Repeat Steps 2 and 3 until you have the required number of stitches.

Cable Cast-On

This firm cast-on, is great for projects requiring a strong, stable edge. It is also useful when adding stitches to an existing row of knitting, as in the picot edging on the Snow Queen Coat.

1. Make a slipknot 6–10" (15–25cm) from the end of the yarn and put the slipknot on a needle.
2. Place the needle in your left hand and put your left index finger over the top of the slipknot to hold it in place. Pick up the other needle with your right hand. Insert the tip of the right needle into the front of the slipknot from left to right, under the left needle and through the stitch.
3. Wrap the working yarn (the yarn in your right hand) around the tip of the right needle by going behind the right needle and working from back to front.
4. Hold the working yarn in your right hand alongside the needle. Bring the right needle to the front by going under the left needle, keeping the wrap on the right needle intact and pulling it through the slipknot. You now have one loop on the right needle and the slipknot on the left needle.
5. Insert the tip of the left needle from left to right through the loop on the right needle and slide the loop from the right to the left needle. Two stitches are now on the left needle and the right needle is empty.
6. Insert the tip of the right needle between the two stitches on the left needle from front to back, under the left needle.
7. Wrap the yarn around the tip of the right needle and pull the wrap of yarn to the front of the work under

the left needle as in Step 4. Slide the new stitch to the left needle as you did in Step 5.
8. Cast on the remaining stitches by inserting the right needle between the two stitches closest to the tip of the left needle as in Step 6 and repeating Step 7.

Chained Cast-On

This cast-on is used to create a temporary or provisional cast-on edge. It is great for those occasions when you want to add trim to your knitting after the piece is finished, such as in the Flower Fairy Cloche. The foundation for this cast-on edge is a crochet chain (see Crochet Techniques in the Special Techniques section) worked over a knitting needle. After the garment is complete, the chain is carefully removed and the resulting live stitches are placed on a knitting needle.

You will need a crochet hook similar in size to the knitting needles required for the project, knitting needles, and smooth cotton waste yarn of comparable weight to the project yarn. Cotton yarn is the best choice for the foundation of this cast-on because it doesn't stretch and is easy to pull out at the end of the project.

1. Make a slipknot 6–10" (15–25cm) from the end of the yarn and place the slipknot on the crochet hook.
2. Hold the knitting needle and the working yarn in your left hand, so that the knitting needle is on top of the working yarn. Hold the crochet hook in your right hand.
3. Cross the hook over the knitting needle so that the end of the hook and the end of the needle form an X.
4. Crochet a chain stitch over the knitting needle and through the loop on the crochet hook. You now have one stitch on the knitting needle and one chain stitch on the crochet hook. Only the stitches on the knitting needle count as cast-on stitches. The single chain stitch that is on the crochet hook is not a cast-on stitch.

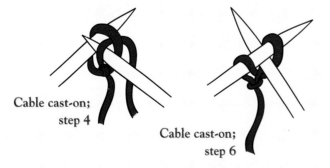

Cable cast-on; step 4

Cable cast-on; step 6

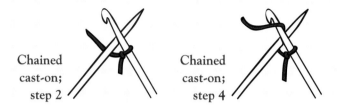

Chained cast-on; step 2   Chained cast-on; step 4

5. Move the knitting needle back into position so that the working yarn is under the needle as in Step 2 and the tips of hook and needle are crossed as in Step 3.

6. Repeat Steps 4 and 5 until you have the desired number of stitches on the knitting needle.

7. To end, cut the yarn, leaving a 6–10" (15–25cm) tail. Remove the loop from the crochet hook and pull the end of the yarn through it. Tie a knot in the end of this tail. Once the knitting is complete and you are ready to work the border, you will begin removing the crochet chain from the knotted end.

The Knit Stitch

This simple stitch is the basis of all knitting. It amazes me still, after years of knitting, that this one stitch is the foundation for everything I have ever learned in knitting. Cables, lace, and countless other techniques start here.

There are several different styles of knitting. English and continental are the two styles that are most commonly used in the United States. The directions that follow are for the English style of knitting. In English knitting you hold the working yarn in your right hand.

The projects in this book can be made successfully with other knitting styles as well. The important thing is that you knit using the style that works best for you.

1. Cast on the required number of stitches.

2. Place the needle with the cast-on stitches in your left hand and hold the working yarn and the other needle in your right hand. The working yarn should be held in back of both needles.

3. Insert the right needle into the front of the first stitch on the left needle, working from left to right and passing the right needle under the left needle. Your needles are now crossed and the right needle is behind the left needle.

4. Wrap the working yarn around the right needle by going behind the right needle and working from back to front.

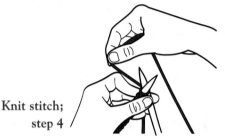

Knit stitch; step 4

5. Hold the working yarn alongside the right needle. Bring the right needle to the front by passing it under the left needle and through the cast-on stitch, keeping the wrap around the right needle as you do so. The needles are now crossed so that the right needle (with the wrap) is in front and the left needle (holding the cast-on stitch) is in back.

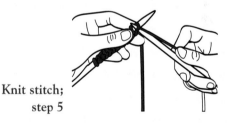

Knit stitch; step 5

6. Slide the right-hand needle to the right so that the cast-on stitch on the left needle slides off the tip of the left needle. You now have one knitted stitch on the right-hand needle.

7. Repeat Steps 3–6 until you have knitted all of the cast-on stitches.

The Purl Stitch

This stitch is basically just the back or flipside of the knit stitch. By combining knit and purl stitches you can create all sorts of designs and textures.

1. Place the needle holding the stitches in your left hand and the working yarn and the empty needle in your right hand.
2. Hold the working yarn in front of the right needle. Insert the right needle into the first stitch on the left needle from right to left, through the front of the stitch. Your needles will now be crossed with the right needle in front of the left.

Purl stitch;
step 2

3. Hold the crossed needles between your left thumb and forefinger. Wrap the working yarn all the way around the tip of the right needle by taking it from the front of the work, back behind the right needle, and back around to the front again.

Purl stitch;
step 3

4. Push the tip of the right needle to the back of the work through the stitch on the left needle, keeping the wrap on the right needle as you do so.

5. Move the right needle away from the left needle so that the stitch on the end of the left needle slides off. You now have one complete purl stitch on the right needle.
6. Bring the working yarn back to the front of the work, between the two needles, and repeat Steps 2–5 for the remaining stitches.

Increases

Increases are made to widen a piece and increase the stitch count. They can be used for shaping a garment and for creating a variety of stitch patterns.

Knit in the Front and Back of the Stitch (kfb)

Knit into the front of the stitch on the left needle, but do not slide it off of the needle (see figure A). Instead, move the right needle around to the back of the work and insert it into the back of the stitch, from right to left, and knit it again (see figure B). Slip the stitch off the needle. Two stitches have been made from one.

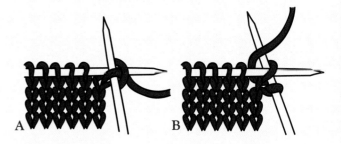

Yarn Over (yo)

This is the simplest of all increases. It increases the stitch count by one each time it is worked and leaves a little hole or eyelet in the fabric. For this reason, it is often used decoratively and in lace patterns.

Bring the yarn to the front of the work between the needles. Place the yarn over the right needle. Work the next stitch, keeping the yarn in place over the right needle as you do so. One yarn over made. On the next row, knit or purl into the yarn over as if it were a normal stitch. You now have one new stitch with a little hole below it.

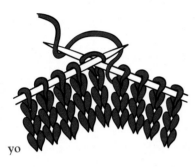

yo

Make One (M1)

This is another very easy way of increasing. It is worked just like the backward loop cast-on (see page 145).

Bring the working yarn to the front of the work and make a backward loop so that the tail crosses over at the right-hand side of the loop. Insert the tip of the right needle into the loop from the cross-over side (the right-hand side) and place it on the needle. The tail of the working yarn will be coming toward you from the base of the new stitch on the right needle. On the next row, knit or purl into this stitch as you would for any normal stitch.

Right Cross Make One (M1R)

This is a great all-purpose increase. It is practically invisible and is always worked between two stitches.

It is often used at the beginning of a row, between the first two stitches. This increase can be a paired increase (two increases worked side-by-side, with one stitch in between) in conjunction with the left cross make one, as in the Mermaid Sun Top.

Locate the horizontal thread that connects the last stitch worked on the right needle and the first stitch on the left needle. Insert the left needle under this thread from back to front, placing it onto the left needle. Knit into the front of this new stitch. You now have one new stitch on the right needle (see figure).

M1R

Left Cross Make One (M1L)

Like the right cross make one, this increase is always worked between two stitches. This increase is often used at the end of a row.

Insert the tip of the left needle from front to back under the thread between the last stitch worked and the first stitch on the left needle. Knit into the back of this picked-up stitch and slide the new stitch off onto the right needle.

M1L

Decreases

Like increases, decreases are used to shape your knitting and for creating patterns. Decreasing narrows your work and reduces the stitch count by one or more stitches.

Knit 2 Together (k2tog)

This is the most basic of all decreases. It produces a single stitch that leans slightly to the right. It is used most often at the end of a row.

To work this decrease, knit the next two stitches on the left needle together by inserting the tip of the right needle into the front of both stitches at once from left to right. Knit the two stitches off the needle as you would normally. One stitch is made from two (see figure on next page).

k2tog

Knit 2 Together Through the Back Loop (k2tog tbl)

This decrease is worked like a normal k2tog except that you are working into the back loops of the stitches. This decrease slants slightly to the left.

With the working yarn at the back of the work, insert the right needle into the back loops of the next two stitches on the left needle, working from right to left. Wrap the yarn around the right needle and knit the two stitches as if they were one. You now have one new stitch on the right needle—one stitch eliminated.

Purl 2 Together (p2tog)

This decrease is worked exactly like k2tog, except that you purl instead of knit. This decrease slants slightly to the right and reduces the stitch count by one stitch. It is used most often at the end of a row.

Bring the working yarn to the front of the work, between the two needles. Insert the right needle into the next two stitches on the left needle from right to left and purl them off as one stitch.

Purl 2 Together Through the Back Loop (p2tog tbl)

Similar to k2tog tbl, this decrease is just like a normal p2tog except that you are working into the back loops of the stitches.

With the yarn at the front of the work, insert the right needle into the back loops of the next two stitches on the left needle, working from left to right. Wrap the yarn around the right needle as you would to purl. Purl the two stitches together as if they were one stitch. One stitch as been made from two.

Slip, Slip, Knit (ssk)

This decrease is the mirror image of k2tog. It is worked on the knit side of the work and produces a left-slanting stitch. Slip, slip, knit decreases the stitch count by one stitch. It is often used at the beginning of a row.

Insert the right needle into the front of the first stitch on the left needle from left to right as if you were going to knit it. Slip this stitch onto the right needle. Repeat with the next stitch on the left needle. You now have two stitches on the right needle. Insert the left needle from left to right into the front of these two stitches as if they were one. Knit them together from this position, wrapping the yarn around the right needle at the back of the work and sliding the new single stitch off the left needle.

ssk

Slip, Slip, Purl (ssp)

This decrease is similar to ssk, although it is worked on the purl side of the work. It decreases the stitch count by one stitch, slants to the left and is often used at the beginning of a row.

Slip two stitches from the left to the right needle, one at a time, as if to knit. Slide the stitches back to the left needle by inserting the left needle into the stitches from left to right. Insert the right needle from left to right through the back of the stitches as if they were one, keeping the right needle at the back of the work. Purl the two stitches together from this position.

Purl 3 Together (p3tog)

This decrease is usually worked on the purl side of the work. It reduces the stitch count by two stitches.

Bring the working yarn to the front, between the needles. Insert the right needle into the front of the next three stitches on the left needle from right to left as if they were one. Purl these three stitches together. One stitch is made from three.

Slip, Knit, Pass Slipped Stitch Over (skpo)

This decrease reduces the stitch count by one.

Slip the first stitch on the left needle to the right needle as if to knit. Knit the next stitch on the left needle. Insert the tip of the left needle into the slipped stitch on the right needle from left to right and pass it over the knit stitch.

skpo

Slip, Knit 2 Together, Pass Slipped Stitch Over (sk2po)

This decrease is also known as a central chain decrease. It is similar to skpo, but it incorporates three stitches leaving a single raised stitch. When worked with paired increases it creates a zigzag pattern as seen in the Princess Crown.

Slip the next stitch from the left to the right needle as if to knit. Knit the next two stitches on the left needle together as one. You now have the slipped stitch and the k2tog stitch on the right needle. Insert the tip of the left needle into the slipped stitch and pass it over the k2tog and off the needle. The k2tog stitch remains on the right needle—one stitch made from three.

Slip, Purl 2 Together, Pass Slipped Stitch Over (sp2po)

This decrease is similar to sk2po. It reduces the stitch count by two stitches.

Slip the first stitch from the left to the right needle as if to knit. Purl the next two stitches together as one. Two stitches are on the right needle, the slipped stitch and the

p2tog stitch. Insert the tip of the left needle into the slipped stitch and pass it over the p2tog and off the needle. The p2tog stitch remains on the right needle—one stitch made from three.

Picking Up Stitches

In many of the patterns in this book you are instructed to pick up stitches along the edge of a knitted piece. This technique offers a seamless way of adding elements, such as sleeves, collars, and edgings, to your knitting.

Unless instructed otherwise, begin with the right side of the fabric facing you. With a needle in your right hand and the working yarn at the back of the work, insert the tip of the right needle from front to back into a selvedge stitch (a stitch at the edge of the knitted fabric). Wrap the yarn around the needle as if to knit and pull the wrap through the stitch to the front of the work. You now have one stitch on the right needle and have just picked up a stitch.

Construction Techniques
Three-Needle Bind-Off

This technique is used to join two knitted edges to one another and bind off stitches at the same time. It is one of my favorite knitting tricks. It creates a smooth, great-looking, and sturdy join without the bulk of a sewn seam. The shoulder seams on many of the outfits in this book are completed with a three-needle bind-off.

This technique is always worked with two sets of live stitches. For most of the projects in this book, each set of stitches is on a separate double-pointed needle. A third needle is required to complete the bind-off.

1. Arrange the work with either right or wrong sides together as directed in the pattern instructions.

2. Place the stitches to be joined on two separate needles. You should have the same number of stitches on each needle. Hold the two needles in your left hand so that they are parallel to one another and the tips of the needles are pointing to the right. Place the third needle in your right hand.

3. Insert the right needle into the front of the first stitch on each of the two needles in your left hand. Wrap the working yarn around the right needle as if to knit and pull the wrap through both stitches. You now have one stitch on the right needle. This is the first stitch on the right needle.

4. Repeat Step 3 so that you have a second stitch on the right needle.

5. Lift the first stitch on the right needle over the second stitch. One stitch remains on the right needle.

6. Repeat Steps 4 and 5 until you have worked across all of the stitches on the needles in your left hand and only one stitch remains on the right needle.

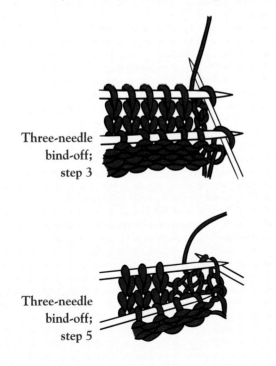

Three-needle bind-off; step 3

Three-needle bind-off; step 5

7. Cut the working yarn, leaving a 6–10" (15–25cm) tail. Thread the tail through the stitch on the right needle and pull it tight to fasten off.

Kitchener Stitch

Also referred to as *grafting*, this technique is used to weave two pieces of knitting together so that they look like one solid piece of fabric. This seaming method is worked with two sets of live stitches, each on a separate needle. The number of stitches on the two needles must be equal for the Kitchener stitch to work.

This technique really fits into the category of knitting magic. It is a little tricky at first, but there is a manageable pattern here and after you have worked through the steps once or twice, it will make more sense. In my experience, the really tricky part of this technique has always come from trying to find my place in the pattern after an interruption. For this reason, I find it best to work through the steps in a quiet place, free from distractions. For the best results, turn off the phone and work this one after the kids have gone to bed.

Kitchener stitch

1. Place the stitches to be joined so that they are evenly divided on two needles.

2. Hold the work in your left hand with the wrong sides of the fabric together. The needles in your left hand should be parallel to one another with one needle in the front and the other in the back. The needle tips should be pointing to the right.

3. This is a preparatory step and will be worked only once. Thread a length of yarn onto a tapestry needle. Holding the tapestry needle in your right hand, insert it into the front of the first stitch on the front needle as if to purl (from right to left) and pull the yarn

through the stitch, leaving a 6–10" (15–25cm) tail at the back of the work. Leave the stitch on the front needle. Next, insert the tapestry needle into the front of the first stitch on the back needle as if to knit (from left to right) and pull the yarn through to tighten it. Leave the stitch on the back needle.

4. Insert the tapestry needle, as if to knit, into the first stitch on the front needle, pull the yarn through, and slide this stitch off the needle.

5. Insert the tapestry needle into the second stitch on the front needle as if to purl. Pull the yarn through the stitch, but do not slide the stitch off the needle; instead, leave this stitch on the needle.

6. Move the tapestry needle around to the back needle. Insert the tapestry needle as if to purl into the first stitch on the back knitting needle. Pull the yarn through and slide the stitch off the knitting needle.

7. Insert the tapestry needle into the second stitch on the back needle as if to knit, pull the yarn through, but leave the stitch on the knitting needle.

8. Repeat Steps 4–7 until you have worked across all of the stitches on the two knitting needles. Here is the mantra that I repeat to myself as I work the Kitchener stitch: Front needle—knit off the needle, purl and leave on. Back needle—purl off the needle, knit and leave on.

9. After all of the stitches have been worked, turn the piece inside out and weave in the ends of the working yarn.

Garter Stitch Seams

This technique forms a vertical and practically invisible seam on garter stitch projects.

1. Thread a tapestry needle with a length of yarn that is approximately twice as long as the seam you need to make. Arrange the pieces to be joined next to one another with the selvedges to be seamed side by side and the right side of the work facing you.

2. Starting at the lower edge of the piece on the right, insert needle into the top loop of the first stitch at the edge of the knitted fabric. Pull the yarn through the loop, leaving a 6–10" (15–25cm) tail.

3. Insert the needle into the bottom loop of the corresponding stitch on the piece on the left and pull the yarn through.

4. Continue working back and forth, working into a bottom loop and then a top loop, right and left, until the seam is complete. Cut the yarn and weave in the ends on the wrong side of the work.

Whipstitch

This is the most basic of all sewing techniques. It is often used on the inside of a garment to sew the hem or facing in place.

Whipstitch

1. Using straight pins, pin the pieces to be joined in place.

2. Thread a tapestry needle with a length of yarn that is twice as long as the seam to be made. Working from the wrong side of the piece, insert the needle into the edge of one of the pieces to be joined and pull the needle through, leaving a 10" (25cm) tail.

3. Insert the needle into the other piece of fabric and pull the yarn through snugly. Continue in this manner, going through both pieces of fabric and working stitches about ¼" (.6cm) apart, until the seam is complete. Fasten the yarn off on the wrong side of the work and weave in the ends.

Short-Rowing

Short-rowing is a way of building up individual sections of your knitting. It adds shape and dimension to a knitted piece and is often used when turning the heel of a sock. You will see this technique in the shawl collar of the Flower Fairy Sweater Coat and the puff sleeves of the Princess Sweater.

When you work short rows, you do not work to the end of the row. Instead, you work to a specified stitch, turn the piece over and work in the opposite direction. When short-rowing, you will be instructed to wrap and turn—**w&t.**

Wrap and Turn (w&t)

1. Work to the place where you are instructed to "w&t the next stitch." Slip the stitch purlwise from the left to the right needle.
2. On knit rows, bring the yarn to the front of the work, between the needles. On purl rows, move the yarn to the back of work, between the two needles.
3. Slip the stitch back to the left needle and turn the work, thus wrapping the slipped stitch. The working yarn is now in place to work the next stitch.

Wrap and turn on knit row

Wrap and turn on purl row

On subsequent rows when you come to a wrapped stitch, pick up the wrap with the tip of the right needle and place it onto the left needle. Work the wrap together with the first stitch on the left needle, knitting the stitch and its wrap together as one. This will hide the wrap and avoid an unwanted hole where the turn was made.

Special Techniques

Decorative Techniques

I-Cord

This technique produces a cord that is both decorative and functional. I-cord is essentially a knitted tube, worked in the round over a few stitches (usually not more than six). It is worked with two double-pointed needles.

I-cord

1. Using double-pointed needles, cast on the number of stitches specified in the pattern.
2. Knit across the stitches. Do not turn work.
3. Slide the stitches to the opposite end of the needle. The yarn will be coming off the left side of the work. Pull the working yarn across the back of the work so that it is at the right side of the work and knit across the row. This brings the two ends together and closes the tube.

Repeat Step 3 until the cord is the length desired. To fasten off the I-cord, bind off the stitches, cut the yarn and pull it through the last stitch.

Pompoms

To make a pompom, you will need a piece of cardboard that is 3" (7.5cm) square, yarn to make the pompom, a 10" (25cm) strand of yarn for tying the pompom, scissors, and a tapestry needle.

Pompom; step 3

Pompom; step 5

1. Wrap a double strand of yarn around the 3" (8cm) piece of cardboard 40 to 50 times.
2. Carefully remove the yarn from the cardboard keeping the bundle intact.
3. Tie the 10" (25cm) length of yarn tightly around the center of the bundle and secure it with a knot.
4. Holding the ends of the center tie, cut the looped ends of the bundle.
5. Still holding on to the center strands, fluff up and trim the bundle so that it is spherical.
6. Attach the pompom by threading the center strands through a tapestry needle and sewing it in place as instructed in the pattern.

Tassels

Before you make a tassel, you'll need a piece of cardboard that is 4" (10cm) wide and long enough to hold comfortably, yarn to make the tassel, two 12" (30cm) strands of yarn for tying the tassel, scissors, and a tapestry needle.

NOTE: The directions that follow are for a two-color tassel. If you would like a solid-color tassel, double the number of wraps in Step 1 and omit Step 3.

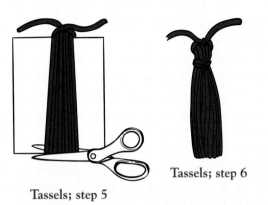

Tassels; step 5

Tassels; step 6

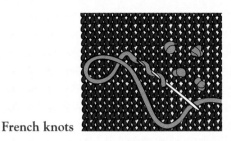

French knots

1. Wrap yarn 50 times around the cardboard, layering it on top of itself as much as possible.
2. Cut the yarn so that the tail end is even with the lower edge of the cardboard.
3. Repeat Steps 1 and 2 for the second color, stacking the yarn on top of itself as much as possible.
4. Take one of the 12" (30cm) strands of yarn and thread it under the yarn bundle at the upper end of the cardboard. Tie a knot tightly around the end of the bundle. Do not cut the ends of this tie; they will be used to sew the tassel onto the knitted piece later.
5. Cut the loops at the lower end of the bundle, and trim to desired length.
6. Wrap the second length of yarn around the entire bundle approximately 1" (3cm) down from the first tie. Tie in place and then turn the bundle over and repeat on the other side. Weave the ends of this tie into the bundle.

French Knots

This embroidery technique works wonderfully on knitted fabric. French knots look like tiny bobbles and are a great way to add a spark of color or texture to your knits. Use them along edges, on collars, or all over to personalize your knits.

1. Thread yarn through a tapestry needle. Begin with the right side of the work facing you. Hold the needle in your left hand at the back of the work. Insert the needle from back to front through the knitted fabric, coming up at the place where you wish to place the French knot. Grab the needle with your right hand and pull the yarn through to the front, leaving a 6" (15cm) tail at the back of the work.
2. With your right hand, hold the needle close to the surface of the fabric at the spot where the needle came out. Use your left hand to wrap the yarn around the shaft of the needle three times.
3. Place your right index finger over the wraps so that they don't slip off the end of the needle. Insert the needle back into the fabric right next to the spot where you pulled it up from the back of the work. Move your left hand back to the WS of the fabric.
4. To make the knot, gently pull the needle from the wrong side of the fabric until the yarn is taut and a knot has formed on the right side of the fabric. As you pull the needle, loosely pinch the wraps between the thumb and forefinger of your right hand. Hold your hand close to the surface of the fabric, as you pull the needle through. The tail of the yarn will pass through the middle of the wraps as you pull the tapestry needle through to the back of the work.
5. If this is the only knot you need to make, cut the yarn and weave the ends in at the back of the work. If you are making a line or group of knots, carry the yarn at the back of the work. Repeat the above steps for remaining knots.

Colorwork

Stripes

When working stripes of four or fewer rows (or rounds), it is helpful to run the yarn up along the wrong side of the work instead of cutting it and joining for each new stripe. To do this, join the yarn at the beginning of each stripe by dropping the color from the last stripe (do not cut it). Bring the new color up and to the left of the dropped yarn. Repeat this for each new stripe, running the yarn up the wrong side of the piece.

Jog-Less Jog

Used in circular knitting, this is a handy trick for avoiding the color jog where a new stripe begins. This technique was developed by knitter/designer Meg Swansen.

Knit the first round of a new stripe. At the beginning of the second round of each new stripe, use the tip of the right needle to pick up the stitch below the first stitch on the left needle (this is the first stitch of the last round). Place this stitch on the end of the left needle and knit it together with the first stitch of the round. Repeating this technique on every second round of a new stripe fuses the stripes together and makes the color switch look smooth and neat.

Intarsia

This is a technique that lends itself well to pictorial knitting. It is usually worked back and forth in rows and allows blocks of color to be scattered on a background of solid or patterned knitting. Each section of color is worked separately, with a separate length of yarn.

Intarsia motifs are generally worked from charts, but this technique may also be used to form color blocks or frame a section of knitting. Intarsia charts are read from the bottom up. On right-side rows they are read from right to left, and on wrong side rows from left to right.

Because you do not carry the yarn across the back of the work when changing colors, you will need to lock the yarns in place to prevent a hole from forming where the color change occurs. To do this on right-side rows, pick up the new yarn from underneath the yarn just used. On wrong-side rows, drop the yarn just used and bring the new yarn up and to the right of the yarn just used. Doing this consistently will twist the yarns together and lock them in place.

Fair Isle

In Fair Isle knitting, the colorwork can be worked in the round or back and forth on rows. This technique is used for colorwork where there is a pattern that is repeated across the row or round. Unlike intarsia knitting, the yarn in Fair Isle knitting is stranded along the wrong side of the work.

Fair Isle knitting is often worked from a chart. The charts are read from the bottom up. If they are worked back and forth in rows, then they are worked from right to left on right-side rows and from left to right on wrong-side rows. When worked in the round, Fair Isle charts are read from right to left for all rounds.

When working Fair Isle, always bring the new color under the one last used. This creates a twist, locking the yarn in place and preventing unwanted holes from forming at the color changes.

Duplicate Stitch

This technique is used to embellish the face of knitted fabric and can be used to imitate intarsia or Fair Isle colorwork. It is used on stockinette fabric to decorate the right side of the work.

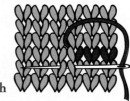

Duplicate stitch

1. Thread a tapestry needle with a length of yarn. Beginning at the back of the work, bring the needle up through the knitting to the right side of the work, so that it comes up at the base of a stitch. Leave a 6" (15cm) tail at the back of the work.

2. Insert the needle under both loops of the base of the stitch directly above the stitch that you want to duplicate.

3. Bring the needle down to the base of the stitch (where you started) and insert it into the knitted fabric, pulling the needle through to the back of the work.

4. Continue to work this way, repeating the above steps and covering the stitches that you want to duplicate.

5. To end, pull the yarn to the wrong side of the work, cut it, and fasten it off.

Crochet Techniques
Chain Stitch

The chain stitch is the foundation of all other crochet stitches. Like knitting, it begins with a slipknot.

Chain stitch

1. Make a slipknot 6" (15cm) from the end of the yarn, and place it on the crochet hook. Pull on the tails of the slipknot so that it sits snugly on the hook.

2. Hold the hook in the right hand and the working yarn in the left. Place your right index finger over the top of slipknot, so that the knot does not slide around on the hook.

3. Wrap the yarn around the hook from back to front, pulling on the working yarn slightly, so that it is taut.

4. Pull the hook through the slipknot, catching the yarn that you wrapped around the hook as you do so. You now have a new loop on the end of the crochet hook and have made one crochet chain.

5. Repeat Steps 2–4 as directed in pattern. Cut the yarn, leaving a 6" (15cm) tail and pull it through the last loop to fasten off the chain.

Slip Stitch

The slip stitch is used in many crochet techniques and is one of the easiest of all crochet stitches. It is often worked into an edge stitch on a knitted piece or into a crochet chain. Slip stitch is used in the picot trim of the Gretel Jumper and the Pirate Dress.

Slip stitch

1. Insert the hook into a stitch as directed in pattern.

2. Wrap the yarn as for a chain stitch, and pull the loop through the stitch. You now have two loops on the hook.

3. Pull the second loop through the first loop, leaving one loop remaining on the hook.

4. Repeat the above steps, as directed in pattern.

Single Crochet

The single crochet stitch is used in almost every other crochet stitch you will ever need. It is used to make the picot trim used in several patterns in this book.

Single crochet; step 2   **Single crochet; step 3**

1. Insert hook into a stitch as directed in pattern.
2. Wrap yarn around hook as to chain and pull it through the stitch. You should have two loops on the hook.
3. Wrap the yarn around the hook again, catching the yarn and pulling it through both loops on the hook. You now have one loop on the hook and have completed your first single crochet.
4. Repeat the above steps, continuing as directed in pattern.

Finishing Techniques
Blocking Your Knitting

Blocking is one of those things about which knitters have very definite opinions. Some knitters always block their work and others never do. I generally block my handknits.

1. Wash the piece with mild detergent, as directed on the yarn label. Rinse. Gently squeeze to remove water.
2. Spread the piece out on top of a thick towel and place another towel on top of it. Roll the towels up like a cinnamon roll and gently squeeze the bundle to remove excess water.

3. Spread a clean towel or blanket on a bed, board, or carpeted area (away from furry friends and the pitter patter of little feet). Using stainless steel pins, pin the piece to the towel/blanket and the blocking surface.
4. Let air dry. When the piece is dry, turn it over and allow it to dry on the other side as well.

NOTE: Sometimes it isn't necessary to wash the piece right after you knit it. For those occasions, mist the piece with clean water and a plant mister. When the piece is nice and damp, proceed to Step 2 and work through the remaining steps.

Facings

The hem, neckline and center openings of some of the projects in this book are reinforced with a ribbon facing. Facings provide added body and structure to garments. This is especially nice for garments that will get a lot of wear or are made with loosely spun yarn. Facing can also be used for decorative purposes. Adding a ribbon facing to your work is optional. To make a facing, cut a length of ribbon or bias tape 1" (3cm) longer than the area you wish to cover. Pin the ribbon to the inside of the garment so that the right side of the ribbon is facing you. Fold the raw ends under so that they are hidden from view, and sew the ribbon facing in place.

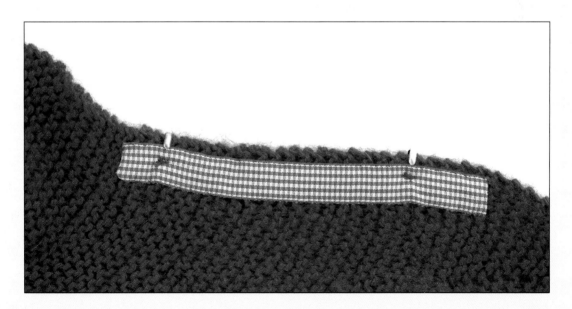

Felting

Place the knitted piece in a zippered pillowcase or mesh laundry bag. Put the bag into a washing machine with hot water and a small amount of detergent. Add a pair of jeans or similar item to the washer tub to create more friction and help facilitate the felting process. Turn the washer on and allow it to complete the wash cycle, stopping it before it progresses to the rinse cycle. Open the bag containing your knitting and check the felting. If the piece is not felted enough, place it back in the bag and reset the washer to the agitation portion of the wash cycle. It is a good idea to open the bag and check the progress of the felting every 5 minutes or so. Repeat as necessary, stopping when your piece is the density and size desired. Now that your piece is sufficiently felted, remove it from the washer, squeeze out the excess soapy water over a sink, and rinse by hand in warm water. Return the piece to the washer and spin the excess water out of it (just spin—no agitation). Remove from the washer.

Blocking Your Felting

The final step in the felting process is blocking. This is especially important for items like the Pirate Messenger Bag and the Elf Slippers and Stocking.

Gently pull the piece into the shape desired. Drying your felted piece over a form helps it maintain its shape. Plastic bags can be used to make a good form. Stuff the bags into the piece, gently pushing and pulling the felt in to the desired shape. Boxes or books placed inside a plastic bag make a great form for felted items like the Pirate Messenger Bag. Place them inside the bag. Let the piece air dry, turning it periodically so that it dries on all sides. Once the outside is dry, take the form out of the piece so that the inside dries as well.

Index

About the Author

Alison Stewart-Guinee is a knitter, weaver, and teacher of textile classes and workshops. Knitting and designing for children is the perfect fit for this mom and former teacher. Strongly influenced by ethnic textiles and traditional knitting techniques, she approaches knitting from a sculptural perspective with an emphasis on color, stitch pattern, and seamless construction. Alison teaches knitting, needlepoint, weaving, and dyeing workshops to adults and children throughout the U.S. and at her local yarn store, Yarns Unlimited in Bloomington, Indiana. She has published designs in several knitting publications including *Charmed Knits*, *Find Your Style and Knit It Too*, and *Not Your Mama's Knitting*. She is currently working on a line of patterns for children and the home, which can be found at www.knittingbyhand.com. When not knitting or teaching, she weaves a line of art-to-wear scarves sold through galleries and juried art fairs. Alison lives in central Indiana with her husband and three children. You can follow her adventures with sticks and string at www.alisonguinee.blogspot.com. *Fairy Tale Knits* is her first book.

Special Thanks to the following companies for their generosity in providing yarn for the projects in this book:

Cascade Yarns, www.cascadeyarns.com
Knit Picks, www.knitpicks.com
Lion Brand Yarns, www.lionbrand.com
Plymouth Yarn, www.plymouthyarn.com
Tahki/Stacy Charles, Inc. (supplier of
    Tahki and Filatura di Crosa yarns),
    www.tahkistacycharles.com

Free Patterns Available Online

Download two additional *Fairy Tale Knits* patterns at www.wiley.com/go/fairytaleknits.